give us today our DAILY BREAD

JANUARY | FEBRUARY | MARCH 2025

Give Us Today Our Daily Bread - January, February, and March 2025

The UNIVERSITY BIBLE FELLOWSHIP is an international evangelical church. Our focus is to help college students to study the Bible and live according to its teachings. We labour and pray to raise lifelong disciples of Jesus among college students who trust in Christ and seek to live by his grace, obeying his commandments (e.g., Jn 13:34; Mt 28:18-20). UBF serves world evangelism by raising lay missionaries and sending them throughout the world.

UBF is a member of Evangelical Council for Financial Accountability, Missio Nexus, Evangelical Missiological Society, MissionExcellence, Kingdom Inter-Missions Network, and Korea Evangelical Fellowship.

Book Design: UBF Press

6540 N. Artesian Ave., Chicago IL 60645

Website: https://ubfpress.org

Email: ubfpress@gmail.com

HOW TO USE DAILY BREAD?

1. **PRAYER:** Before reading the word of God, let us prepare our minds with prayer. "I seek you with all my heart; do not let me stray from your commands"(Psalm 119:10)

2. **READING:** What does the message say? Notice the facts carefully so that we may know what the word actually says.

3. **THINKING:** What does it mean? What is the meaning which the author is seeking to convey?

   Notice especially:

   a. Teachings about God the Father, His only Son Jesus and the Holy Spirit.
   b. Teachings to be followed in the Christian life: **Promises** to believe and claim/ **Commands** to be obeyed / **Warnings** to be heeded / **Habits** to be changed / **Sins** to be avoided.
   c. What is (are) the important thing(s) of this passage?
   d. Think about the key verse (memorize if possible)

4. **WRITING:** Summarize in writing the content and meaning of the passage, and write briefly how it applies to you in your own situation.

5. **PRAYER:** Conclude by writing your own prayer based on the passage. Write your own one word.

give us today our

DAILY BREAD

JANUARY, FEBRUARY, AND MARCH 2025

CONTENTS

"ENTER HIS GATES WITH THANKSGIVING
AND HIS COURTS WITH PRAISE;
GIVE THANKS TO HIM AND PRAISE HIS NAME."

PSALMS 100:4

Authors

Jacob Kim (Isaiah 49:1-7; Genesis 1-3)
Christine Butcher (Genesis 4-8)
Joy King (Genesis 9-17)
Joe Wert (1 Kings 12:16-16:34;
Haggai 1-2; Obadiah 1)
Jason Perry (1 Kings 17-22)
Yvonne Lee (Daniel 1-12)
Steve Stasinos (Genesis 18-24)
David Miller (2 Kings 1-5)
Paul Lee (2 Kings 6-11)

Editors & Proofreaders

Grace Baik
Esther Kim
Tony King

January

Sun	Mon	Tue	Wed	Thu	Fri	Sat
29	30	31	1	2	3	4
5	6	7	8	9	10	11
12	13	14	15	16	17	18
19	20	21	22	23	24	25
26	27	28	29	30	31	1

REACHES TO THE ENDS

Isaiah 49:1-7
Key Verse 49:6

This passage is a Messianic prophecy. It talks of a "servant of the Lord" who is a reflection of our Lord Jesus. The Israelites have been living in oppression and exile, like a lowly tribe among mighty empires of the world. However, this word of the Lord brought a message of hope and deliverance. This hope is for you and for me, and to those at the very ends of the earth. The ends of the earth are not just the Gentiles, but those we may never have imagined God saving. The gospel is often considered offensive not because of those it excludes, but because of those it welcomes.

Jesus spent his limited time on earth with those on the margins of society including the lower class, women, the sick and demon possessed, children, racial minorities, outcasts and public sinners. The gospel very quickly became a message of salvation to all people because God's heart and love extends to all who are suffering and feel excluded. Such grace was offensive to those in power, but it has power to change the world.

Prayer: Father, thank you for extending grace and salvation to me. May this grace overflow and expand in my heart to the very ends.

One Word: God's salvation reaches to the ends.

IN THE BEGINNING

Genesis 1:1-5
Key Verse 1:3

The earth was formless, empty, and dark. Even then, the Spirit of God hovered over the waters. God used words to create something out of nothing. With His word, God brought to the world light, life, beauty, and meaning into existence.

God said, "Let there be light." God distinguished the light from darkness, day from night. With light came the first break of dawn. It was the dawn of something good and very bright.

Although we normally think of the start of our days in the morning, each day of creation starts with evening and ends with the morning. It reveals God who works to bring light and clarity from chaos and darkness. In the same way, our lives may be a reflection of God's work. If things are dark and chaotic, we can trust in God's creation power for light and hope at the end of the day.

Prayer: Father, may the light of your love and grace dawn in my life.

One Word: Let there be light.

THE WONDERS OF CREATION

Genesis 1: 6 -25
Key Verse 1:12

These passages describe God who created the world and everything in it: The sky (day 2), land, sea, and vegetation (day 3), the solar system (day 4), the birds and fish (day 5), and finally all the creatures of the land (day 6).

As a civilization we have marveled at God's creation. Scientists have studied the farthest reaches of space and examined the tiniest of atoms. Artists have written or portrayed the beauty and wonder of nature. We still stand in awe at the beauty, order, and depth of nature. The Apostle Paul wrote that God's invisible qualities, his eternal power and divine nature are revealed in creation (Rom 1:20). And the Psalmist wrote "The heavens declare the glory of God" (Ps 19:1).

While the Bible itself is not a science book, all of our studies of the world come from a place of wonder and awe in his creation. In the midst of our struggles, we can come to God by just looking up to the stars or opening our eyes to nature as we take a walk in the park. Suddenly our problems don't seem so huge. Somehow, the God who holds the universe together, can hold us in his grace and power.

Prayer: Creator God, you hold the depth and beauty of nature in your mind. We seek you in awe, wonder, and joy.

One Word: Experience the glory of God in nature.

IN THE IMAGE OF GOD

Genesis 1:26-31
Key Verse 1:27

On the sixth day, God made mankind in his own image. Each and every person bears the image of God. Whether one is a man or woman, Jew or Palestinian, conservative or liberal, Black or White, straight or gay, rich or poor, or any other variety of human being, each person bears the image of God that cannot be taken away from them.

When we choose to see each and every person as a child of God, rather than a stereotype, we can begin to seek that which is holy and worthy of love and respect in each person. We can start listening to each other with empathy, collaborating, and caring for those in need. Jesus said, "Whatever you did for one of the least of these brothers and sisters of mine, you did for me" (Mt 25:40).

God is love, and each person is made to love and be loved. In God's love, he entrusted us with the beauty and riches of the earth to grow and fill the earth and be good stewards of all of His creation.

Prayer: Creator God, I am your child and image bearer whom you love and delight in. Help me to love all your creation with your love bestowed on me.

One Word: It was very good.

REST

Genesis 2:1-7
Key Verse 2:3

God finished creating the heavens and the earth in six days. On the seventh day he rested. God blessed this day and made it holy. Jesus said that God created the Sabbath for mankind (Mk 2:27). God knows that rest is necessary for us, and for all of creation.

Rest does not just mean having a day off work, but it may mean unplugging from social media and from anything that distracts us from true rest, where we can truly appreciate God and everything that He created. It is an intentional practice of being present with God, others, and oneself. What does rest look like for a parent who cannot simply pause everything? What does it mean to you?

Man was made from the dust of the ground and the breath of God. We are both physical and spiritual beings. We need both food and the word of God. We need both physical and spiritual rest.

Prayer: Creator God, you rested on the seventh day. May we seek true rest that you provide in body, mind, and spirit.

One Word: Rest.

CARE FOR THE GARDEN

Genesis 2:8-17
Key Verse 2:15

After creating the universe, the earth, and everything in it, God created a beautiful garden and put the first man Adam there to take care of it. God gave him everything he needed to survive. All of God's beautiful creation on earth was his life's work to care for.

God still calls us to be stewards of the earth and to care for it as our home while we are living in it. All of creation reveals God's glory. When we are connected to nature, in even small ways, we can experience the wonder of God. How can I be a good steward of this earth that God has put me in? How can I preserve this earth for future generations? Whether in big or small ways, we can take part in enjoying and caring for this world that God has put us in.

Prayer: Creator God, the beauty and life-giving resources of the earth sustain me. May I enjoy it and care for it.

One Word: Be a good steward of your garden.

TOGETHER WITHOUT SHAME

Genesis 2:18-25
Key Verse 2:25

God saw that even with all the beauty and sustenance the earth provided man, and even though work could keep him busy for a very long time, it was not good for the man to be alone. God created man, in his own image, to be in relationship with others, just as God is in relationship with us and the Son and the Holy Spirit.

While pets can offer some meaningful companionship, there is nothing like another human being to share our joys and our sorrows with. We are made to love, and love requires an intimate relationship. Love is the giving and receiving of one another without shame.

God created woman from Adam's own rib and united them as one flesh. They were both naked and felt no shame. Each of them saw each other for who they truly are, without pretense, without trying to impress or prove their worthiness for each other. They accepted each other with gratitude in being able to share life and their garden home together.

Prayer: Creator God, you are the source of love that we may radiate to others with a genuine and open heart.

One Word: Accept each other in love.

SIN AND SHAME

Genesis 3:1-13
Key Verse 3:9

There was just one restriction God gave Adam and Eve: to not eat from the tree of the knowledge of good and evil. But it was right there, and it looked pleasing. With the temptation of the crafty serpent, the fruit called out to Adam and Eve to try it. They both ate of it and suddenly felt shame. Although we may blame the serpent, Adam, or Eve, we are no better or worse. This is a depiction of sin and shame that we all experience in our lives.

Shame is defined as that intensely painful feeling of humiliation caused by the realization of wrong or foolish behavior. Sin leads to shame and causes us to believe that we are no longer acceptable to God or others. Adam and Eve realized they were naked and felt like they had to cover themselves. Shame makes us uncomfortable in our own skin. When confronted by God, they both hid and blamed others. Shame makes us hide and blame others. Shame feels a lot like hell and death, but God did not abandon them in their shame. He sought them.

Prayer: Creator God, I have sinned against you and others, yet you never gave up on me.

One Word: God is still seeking you in love.

A CURSED WORLD

Genesis 3:14-24
Key Verse 3:19

The consequence of sin was death. It was also hardship, struggle, and pain. What was once perfect became tainted. Once they were naked and felt no shame, now they had to dress to impress or to hide their shame. Once they loved and accepted each other as they were, now cursed desires and power struggles arose in their relationships. Once they found the simple pleasures in life, now they had to work for life's necessities.

For sure, we still live in a fallen world, full of sin and hardship. But God did not abandon us. God's salvation was always in mind. It is said the first prophecy of Jesus is here, that speaks of the offspring of woman crushing the head of the serpent. God did not intend to leave us in our brokenness, but to be with us in it, and to restore us to himself and to each other. Adam could still choose to love his wife instead of rule over her and seek God's kingdom and righteousness despite hardships. The tree of life, though out of reach, remained.

Prayer: Creator God, we are accountable for our sins, yet you are with us through it. May we experience your saving grace.

One Word: God is with us in our struggle.

CAIN AND ABEL

Genesis 4:1-15
Key Verse 4:7

After the fall, Adam and Eve bore two sons, Cain and Abel. Abel kept flocks, while Cain worked the soil. Both brought an offering to God in the course of time. Hebrews 11 tells us that, by faith, Abel brought a better offering than Cain (Heb 11:4). God favored Abel's offering but not Cain's. Are our offerings and actions before God done in faith?

Cain became angry and downcast that he did not receive God's favor. But the LORD instructed him that if he did what was right, he would also be accepted. He also warned Cain, knowing that anger resided in Cain's heart, that if he did not do what was right, sin would master him. Sadly, Cain did not listen or repent, and his anger led him to kill his brother Abel. As a result, he was driven away from the LORD's presence and became a restless wander on the earth.

There are consequences for our unrepented sin. We must learn to master our sinful will and desires through confession and repentance. One key way to do this is by humbly responding to God's words. When we repent by heeding His word, we can master the sin in our hearts and walk in the light.

Prayer: Father, we confess our unrepented and hidden sin, our false motives, jealousy, pride, and fear to You. May we heed Your words and warning to do what is right.

One Word: Learn to do what is right

CALL UPON THE NAME OF THE LORD

Genesis 4:16-26

Key Verse 4:26b

Cain left the LORD's presence. He married and had a son and built a city. His descendants became farmers, musicians, and tool makers. Although this seems successful and productive, we see that sin continued to reign in Cain's bloodline through polygamy, murder, and violence. Without God in our lives—no matter what we do, have, or achieve—sin will remain.

Amid a growing culture of godlessness, God granted Adam and Eve another son, and they named him Seth. In turn, Seth had a son and named him Enosh, which means, "mortal, human, and weak." During this time, people began to call on the name of the LORD.

We are living in a culture of increased and growing godlessness. How do we respond? Like the people in Enoch's time, we can be those who call on the name of the Lord out of our desperate need for him.

Prayer: Lord, as humans we can do so much apart from You, but we confess that we are in need of You. We are living in desperate times where many live apart from You. Make us a people who will call upon Your name.

One Word: Call upon the name of the Lord

ENOCH

Genesis 5:1-32
Key Verse 5:24

God created mankind in his own likeness. But due to the fall, mankind became mortal. This meant that they lived, had children, and then died. It was the cycle of life. However, one man's story distinctly stands out. Enoch was a man who walked faithfully with God. He lived a total of 365 years and was then no more because the LORD took him away. He was a friend of God.

Lamech had a son and named him Noah, which means comfort. After the fall, life became hard and toilsome. But Lamech put his hope in the Lord that He would bring comfort. God is the giver of all comfort.

In this life, where we work hard to eat and survive, we too can put our hope in the LORD. We can live to walk with God faithfully.

Prayer: Father, I want to be someone who walks faithfully with you all the days of my life..

One Word: Be a friend of God.

Monday, January 13

NOAH WALKED FAITHFULLY WITH GOD

Genesis 6:1-22
Key Verse 6:9b

God created a beautiful world for man. But, after sin entered, man turned his heart away from Him. Not only did people become flesh and marry and live as they pleased, but also the thoughts of their hearts were only evil all the time. They became enemies of God. The earth became corrupt because man corrupted his ways. The LORD's heart was grieved, and he regretted that He made mankind- so much so that He was going to wipe away the human race from the face of the earth. We must remember how our sin deserves punishment because it grieves God's heart.

In spite of the corruption of the world, there was one person named Noah who was righteous and walked faithfully with God. He did not pursue the favor of man, but he found favor with God. Noah lived in obedience to the LORD. In holy fear, he built an ark as God commanded (Heb 11:7) to save himself and his family. We get a glimpse of what was to come: Those who obey God's words by putting their faith in Christ would also be saved. We also can build our lives in reverence to God and be set apart for Him in our modern time.

Prayer: Father, our sin and rebellion grieve your heart. May we walk humbly before You and be set apart for our generation to bring others to You to be saved.

One Word: Walk by faith before God and be set apart

THE FLOOD

Genesis 7:1-24
Key Verse 7:23

The LORD found Noah righteous in his generation. He told Noah to take his whole family, as well as every kind of animal and bird, clean and unclean, into the ark. After seven days, the LORD was going to send rain on the earth for forty days and forty nights and wipe away, from the face of the earth, every living creature. Noah did all that the LORD commanded.

The floodwaters came to earth, and for forty days, the flood kept rising on the earth. Every living thing that moved on the ground perished. But Noah, and all who were with him in the ark, were saved. Noah's life, obedience, and faith not only spared himself, but his entire family and those that followed. Our lives of faith can bear fruit for others to be saved. This passage illustrates what God ultimately did for mankind. We each deserve punishment because of our wickedness, rebellion, and sin. But God gave His One and Only Son Jesus Christ so that those who would believe in him would not perish but be saved and receive eternal life (Jn 3:16).

Prayer: Father, thank you for saving me from eternal judgement by sending Your Son. May I live by faith and obedience to You alone. Even through my own life, may many others put their faith in Jesus and be saved.

One Word: Live by faith and be saved through Jesus Christ

GOD REMEMBERED NOAH

Genesis 8:1-22
Key Verse 8:21

The earth was covered with water. The people and animals were gone. God sent a great wind, and the waters receded. After ten months, the tops of the mountain became visible. Then after forty days, Noah sent a raven, and then a dove, to see if the water had receded. The dove found nowhere to perch, and so Noah waited seven more days. Then the dove returned with an olive leaf. Noah had to wait a long time, but God remembered him.

When Noah was 601 years old, the LORD told him and his family to leave the ark, along with all of the living creatures. It was a new beginning. While everyone on the earth had perished, Noah and his family were saved. In response, Noah built an altar to the LORD out of gratitude, reverence, and deep thankfulness. Then the LORD said in His heart that He would never again curse the ground or destroy the living creatures, even though He knew man was sinful. He instead gave us His One and Only Son Jesus Christ. In Him, we too can have a new beginning and life, and not because of anything we have done, but because our sin has been washed away through his blood shed on the cross for us.

Prayer: Father, thank you for remembering us. Though we are evil, You spared us and gave us your Son so we may have a new life and live eternally with You. May we build an altar of thanksgiving every day for what You have done.

One Word: God kept His covenant with mankind through His Son Jesus Christ

GOD GAVE MEN A SIGN OF THE COVENANT

Genesis 9:1-17
Key Verse 9:17

God's blessing to Noah and his sons appears to be the same one given to Adam in the beginning of creation (Gen 1:28-30). However, there are some changes. After the flood, the environment changed, and mankind needed to consume the meat of animals in addition to plants for food. God allowed them to eat meat for their physical needs but on one condition: they were not to consume the blood that represented life. Also, shedding human blood was prohibited because the image of God—life itself—in each person belongs to God.

Through the flood, God demonstrated his power and authority as the author of all lives and judge. God deserves our absolute respect and submission. Yet, he does not want to have a relationship based on fear. God also made a covenant with Noah, promising not to destroy the earth with a flood again, and gave the sign of the rainbow. God's covenant does not mean the world, as we know it, will last forever (2Co 4:18). Rather, the covenant is God's commitment to his creatures that he will endure, patiently guide, and be faithful to his words. It is God's grace to commit and hold to his promises. Do you also want to commit your life to God and follow his words?

Prayer: Father, you are gracious and faithful. I want to be faithful to you and obey your will. Would you be with me today to have the strength to be right with you?

One Word: God made a covenant

NOAH AND HIS SONS AFTER FLOOD

Genesis 9:18-29
Key Verse 9:19

Noah went back to his old job and planted a vineyard. Perhaps he had a good harvest, because the Bible records him sleeping naked, drunk from the wine from his vineyard. When Ham saw his father Noah being indecent, Ham left Noah there and told his brothers, embarrassing Noah further. But Shem and Japheth had more respect for Noah than their brother. They entered the room and covered Noah without seeing his nakedness.

When Noah woke up and found out what had happened, he cursed Ham's son Canaan to be a slave of his brothers. Here, Ham is referred to as "the father of Canaan." It implies that Ham would not set a good, moral example as an ancestor, therefore, influencing his descendants to wickedness (Dt 9:5). Ham could blame Noah for this outcome—after all, Noah was indecent first, causing Ham to disrespect him. Yet, we each are accountable for our actions that we choose every moment of our lives. Experiencing and surviving the fatal flood did not make Noah and his sons holy. However, just as God had blessed them, God then raised people to fill the earth. Will you choose to live by the words of our faithful Father, overcoming pride and the temptations of the world?

Prayer: Father, thank you for teaching us what is right and wrong. I want to share in your heart to see right and wrong clearly and make the right decision each moment.

One Word: Be right before God

DESCENDANTS OF SHEM, HAM, AND JAPHETH

Genesis 10:1-32
Key Verse 10:32

Chapter 10 lists the names of each of Noah's three sons' descendants (5) beyond the account of chapter 11. This chapter also explains Genesis 9:19. Many of the sons' names represent the kingdoms that their descendants later established and the regions they occupied.

Among them, Nimrod, a descendant of Ham, was known as a "mighty hunter before the LORD" (8), meaning he was known to be mighty on earth—and opposed the LORD above. He claimed the territory from Shinar, where Babel stood, to Assyria, where he built the great cities of Nineveh and Calah. While Ham's descendants seemed to prosper despite the curse of his father Noah, God was raising the children of Japheth and Shem as well. God fulfilled his blessing for them to "increase in number and fill the earth" (9:1) with full provision.

People want to plan their own way and make their name known according to their pride. Yet God's purpose for us is clear: through the history of human affairs, we will seek him and come to know him better (Acts 17:26-27).

Prayer: Father, you faithfully provide for us and keep your promise. I want to fix my eyes on you today so that I may not be lost in the rumors and news of the world but see how you consistently carry out your plans and blessings.

One Word: The nations spread out over the earth

THE LORD SCATTERED THEM

Genesis 11:1-32
Key Verse 11:9b

When people settled eastward in the plain in Shinar (2, 10:10), with the benefit of everyone speaking one language, they conspired to go against God's will. They wanted to build a city with a tower reaching the heavens. Their desire to make a name for themselves resembles Eve's desire to become like God (Ge 3:5,6). Instead of living according to God's blessing to subdue the world and be stewards of God's creation, they desired to reach God with their wits.

So, God confused their language to stop the project, and they were scattered. Those who understand modern science and technology know the plan of the people of Babel was ridiculous. While they were setting themselves up for failure, God redirected them to go out and conquer the world, fulfilling his will. God already knew every inclination of human thoughts was evil (6:5). They knew no boundaries in conspiring against God (6).

God showed his love and grace by confusing their language and stopping their self-destructive work. God's plan would not stop there. He was raising one man from Shem's descendants who would establish a covenant relationship with him.

Prayer: Father, you are almighty and in control. You do not waver by human conspiracy. I pray for your will to be done on earth. I belong to you. Please use me for your good purpose.

One Word: God fulfills his will

CALL OF ABRAM

Genesis 12:1-9
Key Verse 12:3b

The last part of chapter 11 gives a brief history of Abram's family. His father Terah, from Chaldea, set out to go to Canaan with his sons and their wives. They settled mid-way at Harran.

Chapter 12 introduces God's calling of Abram, who did not have much significance until then. God commanded him to leave his father's house, the place of comfort, and follow God's guidance to the land of His promise. God's promise for Abram: to make him a source of blessing to all peoples on earth, and whoever curses Abram would bear God's curse (3). God was inviting Abram to leave his comfort zone and take a place on God's side under his protection (Isaiah 41:10).

Abram responded to the call by simply obeying. He took his household and traveled to Canaan as God showed him. Abram was not discouraged by the fact that people already occupied the land. He trusted God's presence (7) and believed the promise that his descendants would occupy the land. Moreover, he understood the weight of God's covenant and cherished the eternal kingdom God would bring to the whole earth, beginning with Abram himself (Heb 11:10).

Prayer: Father, thank you for calling Abram to be a blessing. I pray to respond to your call with my trust in your perfect and good plan.

One Word: So Abram went

GOD DIVIDES ISRAEL

1 Kings 12:16-33
Key Verse 12:19

The king of Israel, Rehoboam, refused to listen to his people when they asked him to be a merciful king. Instead, he promised a hard, uncompromising rule. This alienated most of the rest of the kingdom, and so ten tribes broke off from the tribe of Judah. When Rehoboam sent out Adoniram to put down the rebellion, he was murdered, and the king barely escaped with his own life. After the northern kingdom made Jeroboam king, Rehoboam mustered a huge army to take back the nation. But God warned him not to even try it, as this was from the Lord. The nation of Israel was torn in two, its glory days gone forever. This was a result of the sin of Rehoboam.

The Lord had promised Jeroboam that, if he obeyed his word, the Lord would make an enduring dynasty. But Jeroboam did not value the word of God. When he became king of Israel, he quickly abandoned the word of God and set up convenient places of worship. He made two locations in Israel as places to worship the Lord, and set up a golden calf in both places, so the people wouldn't have to travel to Judah to worship the Lord. He also significantly loosened the qualifications to serve as priest. The nation of Israel was ensnared in sin from the beginning.

Prayer: Father, when we don't value your word, sin is the inevitable result. Help our leaders to hold to your word.

One Word: Leaders must fear God

THE LORD REBUKES JEROBOAM

1 Kings 13:1-10
Key Verse 13:2

Just as quickly as Jeroboam fell into the sin of forming a new religion, God sent his servant to rebuke him. As Jeroboam was standing beside the altar of one of his places of worship, a man of God came and warned him of the terrible consequences of his sin. A man named Josiah would be born in the house of David, and the nation of Israel would be punished severely by God. "On you he will sacrifice the priests of the high places who make offerings here, and human bones will be burned on you." (2) The man of God gave Jeroboam a sign, in case he didn't believe him. The sign was that the altar would be split apart, and ashes would fall out of it. Jeroboam was furious and tried to have the man of God seized, but when he stretched out his hand it was shriveled. Just then, the sign the man of God spoke came true.

King Jeroboam didn't repent. He didn't ask for the restoration of God's mercy on Israel. Instead, he asked for his hand to be healed, which the man of God graciously did. The king then invited the man of God for a meal, but he refused, saying the Lord had commanded him not to eat or drink anything and must not return the way he came. The man of God was absolute with God's word. Jeroboam was careless. His nation would pay the price.

Prayer: Father, thank you for your servants who remind us of your word. Help us to listen to them and repent before it is too late.

One Word: Sin has terrible consequences

GOD'S WORD IS CERTAIN

1 Kings 13:11-34
Key Verse 13:32

An old prophet heard what the man of God had said and done, and he wanted to meet him. So, he went and met the man of God and invited him to come home with him and have something to eat. The man of God refused, saying God had told him not to eat or drink anything in that land. But the old prophet lied to him and said God had told him to bring the man of God back to his home to eat bread and drink water. So the man of God went with him. While eating, the prophet rebuked the man of God for disobeying God's word. The man of God had no discernment. He should have known God never contradicts his own word.

The man of God paid a heavy price for his lack of discernment—on his way home, he was mauled by a lion. The lion didn't eat the man nor the donkey he was riding. He just stood beside the man's body. The old prophet knew that everything he had said to King Jeroboam would come true. He went and took the body and buried it in his own tomb, mourning, "Alas my brother!" Even as Jeroboam heard what had happened to the man of God, he refused to repent of his wicked ways. His sin, as sin always does, led to the downfall and destruction of the house of Jeroboam. The word of the Lord is always certain.

Prayer: Father, thank you for your word and for the certainty of your word. Help us to hold on to your word. Your word is truth.

One Word: God's word will certainly come true

A PROPHECY OF JUDGMENT

1 Kings 14:1-20
Key Verse 14:14

The son of King Jeroboam, Abijah, became ill. So, Jeroboam told his wife to disguise herself and seek out the prophet Ahijah to discover what would happen to the boy. Jeroboam trusted Ahijah, as he was the one who prophesied Jeroboam would become king. Although Ahijah was blind, the Lord helped him to see through her disguise. Ahijah sent Jeroboam's wife back home with two disastrous prophecies. First was the disaster God would bring on the house of Jeroboam. God raised Jeroboam up and gave him much of David's kingdom. But Jeroboam was no David. His sin of idolatry caused God to turn his back on Jeroboam. God would cut off every male in the house of Jeroboam.

The second prophesy was about the death of Jeroboam's son. Ahijah told Jeroboam's wife that their son would die as soon as she stepped across the threshold of her house. As soon as she stepped across the threshold, the boy died. It seemed like very dark times for Israel's future. But God promised that he would raise up a king of Israel who would be zealous for him. Even in the midst of judgment, there is always hope in God.

Prayer: Father, you are sovereign over all things and you judge sin. Help the people of our land to repent before your word, beginning with me.

One Word: God punishes sin

REHOBOAM, KING OF JUDAH

1 Kings 14:21-31
Key Verse 14:22

Rehoboam was King David's grandson and Solomon's son. He had all the advantages anyone could hope for. He knew David's heart for God and Solomon's God-given wisdom. By all accounts he should have been a great king. But he forgot God's grace and he slid into sin. As a nation's leaders go, so goes the nation. Judah also sinned greatly against the Lord. They stirred up the Lord's jealous anger more than any had before them. They engaged in all sorts of idolatry The Lord had set the people of Judah apart from the other nations. They were to be his own. They should have behaved differently from the surrounding nations. They didn't. They ended up adopting the wicked practices of the nations the Lord had told them to drive out.

Egypt attacked Judah and took the temple's treasures, including the gold shields. Rehoboam replaced them with bronze shields. Everything looked the same. But it was all whitewash. Inside, the cup was filthy. Sin corrupted Rehoboam: sin also corrupted the whole nation. Because of this, they were objects of God's wrath.

Prayer: Father, when we forget your grace, we also forget you! Help us to hold on to your word, and to have you in our hearts at all times.

One Word: Hold onto God's word

A WICKED KING AND A GOOD KING

1 Kings 15:1-24
Key Verse 15:14

Rehoboam died, and his son Abijah succeeded him. Like his father before him, Abijah was a wicked king. He likely grew up in a home that did not honor God and his word. So, he committed the same sins his father Rehoboam committed. Throughout his reign, Judah was at war with Israel, their brothers. Abijah reigned only three years. He was not like David, whose heart had been fully devoted to the Lord (except in the matter of Uriah's wife). However, for the sake of his servant David, God kept a lamp burning in Jerusalem by giving Abijah a son. The Lord was faithful to the promise he had made to David to keep a man from his line on the throne for all time.

The lamp God raised up through Abijah was his son Asa. Asa would reign in Jerusalem for forty-one years. He did what was right in the Lord's eyes. He expelled the shrine prostitutes, rid the land of idols, and even deposed his own grandmother when she didn't repent of her idol worship. Asa was not 100% perfect. He did not remove the high places. And he made an alliance with the king of Aram to fight off Israel, instead of trusting in the Lord. Even so, the Lord blessed Judah in battle. Asa's heart, like King David's, was committed to the Lord.

Prayer: Father, help me to commit my heart to you my whole life. May I devote my life to you and your word.

One Word: Be fully committed to the Lord

YOU CAUSED MY PEOPLE TO SIN

1 Kings 15:25-16:14
Key Verse 16:2

Just as King David was the prototype of a king seeking after God's own heart, so King Jeroboam of Israel because the prototype of wicked kings. He became the king that other wicked kings in Israel were compared against. Nadab was a descendant of Jeroboam. Jeroboam set up idol worship in Israel. Nadab followed in that sin and caused Israel to continue idol worship too. God punished him through Baasha. Baasha also killed off everyone left from Jeroboam's family—fulfilling the prophesy God gave to the prophet Ahijah concerning Jeroboam and his whole family. (1KI 14:9,10) But then Baasha, too, fell into idol worship himself. This sin would continue in Israel until God thrust them from his presence.

God then raised up the prophet Jehu to bring judgment on Baasha. Jehu prophesied that the Lord would do to Baasha's family what he had done to Jeroboam's. God had called Jeroboam to lead his people Israel, just as he had called David. But Jeroboam didn't follow in God's ways. He rebelled against God and instituted idolatry and caused God's nation Israel to sin greatly against the Lord. Baasha's son became king when Baasha died. After two years, he was assassinated by Zimri, who became king and killed off all of Baasha's family, fulfilling God's word to Jehu.

Prayer: Father, strengthen us that we may walk in your ways and keep us from the way of sin.

One Word: Walk in the word of the Lord

ISRAEL'S KINGS COMMIT SIN AND DO EVIL

1 Kings 16:15-34
Key Verse 16:18b,19

Zimri had murdered King Elah. He also killed off all of the remaining family of Baasha. The people didn't want a murderer as their king, so they conspired against him and made Omri, the army commander, king. And so, Zimri lasted only seven days before he committed suicide in his palace. He died not because of the conspiracy against him, but because of the sins he had committed against the Lord. Omri was a strong king and built the city of Samaria. However, he too sinned against the Lord. He did more evil in the sight of the Lord than all the other kings had done before him. So he died too.

After Omri died, his son Ahab became king in Israel. Ahab did even more evil than Omri had done. Sin builds up and becomes a completely destructive force, just like a tiny snowball rolled down a mountain can become a massive boulder. Ahab continued to worship idols. He also married Jezebel, the daughter of a Sidonian king. During Ahab's reign, Hiel rebuilt the city of Jericho. According to the Lord's word, it was at the cost of his firstborn and youngest sons. Even when kings are invoking his anger, God is faithful to his word.

Prayer: Father, help us to repent our own idol worship and follow your ways.

One Word: God is always faithful to his word

GOD'S PRESENCE WITH ELIJAH

1 Kings 17:1-24
Key Verse 17:24

To lead Israel to repentance in the time of the wicked king Ahab and Jezebel, the Lord decreed, through the prophet Elijah, an extended drought (1). But Elijah himself lived in Israel. How would he survive? The Lord already had a plan for that (2-6). The time of being fed by ravens was training for Elijah to depend on God and separate himself from the world.

Ultimately, God wanted Elijah not just to survive but to bless others, so Elijah was sent to a widow in Zarephath (7-9). When she showed faith, God miraculously provided for her, her son, and Elijah as well (10-16). However, it seemed Elijah's presence was not enough to prevent tragedy from striking, and the widow's son became ill and died (17-18). But God used this to perform an even greater miracle and verify that Elijah was speaking the words of God (19-24).

In Christ, we are the representatives of God's grace, as Elijah was in his time. First, we need confidence in God's provision so we can overcome self-centeredness. Then, we can be sure that our presence is meant to be a blessing even in times of suffering and loss.

Prayer: Father, thank you for providing for me in good times and bad until this day. Increase my faith that you will use me as a blessing everywhere I go!

One Word: Blessed and a blessing

ELIJAH'S CHALLENGE

1 Kings 18:1-19
Key Verse 18:15

There was one faithful man, Obadiah, in the court of wicked King Ahab. God had used him greatly, to save a hundred of the Lord's prophets from persecution by Jezebel (4,13). Now God wanted to use Obadiah again, to arrange a meeting between Elijah and Ahab (7-8). But this was a new challenge to Obadiah's faith. Elijah was famous for being unpredictable, coming and going at any moment according to the Spirit's leading. Obadiah feared that if Elijah did not show up at the time he promised, Ahab would kill him. But Elijah gave his word that he would be there, and Obadiah obeyed. Ahab and Elijah met at the appointed place and time, and Elijah issued a challenge to the prophets of Baal so all Israel could learn who was really God (19-21).

When we want to do the work of God, we need to work together, which involves depending on and trusting our coworkers. Sometimes this is difficult. But we can overcome doubts by remembering that if we do our part, God will do the rest.

Prayer: Father, thank you for using people like Obadiah in wicked environments. Help me be faithful where I am, and when it's my time to speak up, to find courage.

One Word: A faithful person in a wicked environment.

ELIJAH'S PRAYER

1 Kings 18:20-46
Key Verse 18:37

The people of Israel had all but forgotten their history and calling. Influenced by Jezebel, they fell into Baal worship. The Lord could have left them alone to perish in their sin-blindness. God does not do a miracle to make us remember him every time we forget him. But he used Elijah to open Israel's eyes with a great demonstration that the Lord alone is God who can answer prayer from heaven. After the prophets of Baal did their best with no result, Elijah first gave the people a history lesson (30-31). Then, a miracle happened because of Elijah's earnest prayer to turn the people's hearts back to the Lord (36-37).

God used the boldness and zeal of one person, Elijah, to change a whole generation. We believe he is using people in our generation in the same way. Can the Lord use me like he used Elijah? Yes, if we have a sense of history, deeply understand the spiritual problem of our time, and pray earnestly. Through the burning of the sacrifice and the end of the drought, Israel began to be turned away from Baal worship. May it happen in our times as well.

Prayer: Father, thank you for your grace to call us back to you when we forget you. Please use me to call your people back to you.

One Word: Answer, Lord, and turn our hearts back.

February

Sun	Mon	Tue	Wed	Thu	Fri	Sat
26	27	28	29	30	31	1
2	3	4	5	6	7	8
9	10	11	12	13	14	15
16	17	18	19	20	21	22
23	24	25	26	27	28	1

ELIJAH'S NEXT STEPS

1 Kings 19:1-21
Key Verse 19:18

For a moment, it seemed that Elijah had won a great spiritual victory at Mt. Carmel. But now he had to flee for his life from Jezebel (1-2). Elijah was tempted to despair, asking the Lord to take his life. He blames himself for his apparent lack of success, saying he is no better than his ancestors (3-4). But that was not for Elijah to judge. Elijah had been faithful to the calling God gave him, and that was enough. Now Elijah received personal care from the Lord—a meal and some rest (5-7), and a lesson that the Lord's power is not always shown in big, noisy events (11-13). The Lord assured Elijah that his remnant existed in Israel (18). Then it was time for Elijah to look toward the future, preparing someone else to carry on the work after him (19- 21).

When we feel despair because our work in the Lord seems fruitless, we may just need some physical replenishment. We should also remember that in this world, we never see all the results of our labor in the Lord. When we know that we are very zealous for the Lord, we can be sure he will use our lives in the best way, and we don't need to compare ourselves to others.

Prayer: Father, thank you for your personal care for your servants. Help me do the work you have for me and look to the future as well.

One Word: Rest and prepare the next steps

THE LORD HELPS AHAB

1 Kings 20:1-21
Key Verse 20:13

When Ben-Hadad king of Aram threatened Samaria, Ahab felt he had no strength to oppose him, so he offered to surrender. But when Ben- Hadad then came back with more unreasonable demands, Ahab and his advisors decided to fight back. Ahab and Ben-Hadad then exchanged threats, though Ahab had no true confidence. This event shows the typical nature of human conflict and politics.

At this time the Lord intervened through a prophet and promised to help Ahab defeat Ben-Hadad's army. Ahab did not deserve this grace because of how he and Jezebel persecuted the Lord's prophets, but the Lord did it so that Ahab would learn that the Lord is God, and repent. Ahab was humble enough to ask for the prophet's directions, and by means of the Lord's strategy Ahab inflicted heavy losses on Ben-Hadad.

Let's pray that we may live both courageously and wisely today by listening to good advice from those the Lord sends us. It can make a victory possible where it seemed impossible.

Prayer: Father, thank you for those you graciously send to help me. Help me humbly accept help and win the victory for your name's sake.

One Word: Listen to counsel and be courageous

AHAB'S FOOLISHNESS

1 Kings 20:22-43
Key Verse 20:42

With the Lord's help, Ahab had won a decisive victory over the army of Ben-Hadad king of Aram (20:1-21). The next spring, Ben-Hadad attacked again, and the Lord promised to help Ahab again, to show that he is not just a "God of the hills", but Lord of the whole earth. Ben-Hadad's army was defeated, and Ben-Hadad himself was trapped and about to be captured. When he begged for his life, Ahab welcomed Ben-Hadad as a brother and they made a treaty for mutual benefit. Then the Lord sent a prophet to rebuke Ahab for sparing Ben- Hadad, prophesying that Ahab had forfeited his own life for this sin (42).

Why was it wrong for Ahab to show mercy to Ben- Hadad? It's not genuine mercy when it's for selfish gain. Ben-Hadad had not repented of trying to destroy the Lord's people. Ahab was not a good shepherd and defender of Israel, because he cared about his own prestige and wealth more than those God put under his care. Let's pray that we may be conscious of what God has put under our care and guard it with the mind of a shepherd.

Prayer: Father, please make me a shepherd who will stand up to protect the sheep you put under my care.

One Word: A good shepherd doesn't make a deal with wolves.

WICKEDNESS AND REPENTANCE

1 Kings 21:1-29
Key Verse 21:27

Naboth was a righteous man who kept the Lord's command by refusing to sell his inheritance in Israel (Lev 25:23). Ahab was a selfish, petty man who sulked like a child when he didn't get his way (4b). But Jezebel had no conscience at all. In order to seize Naboth's vineyard, she created a conspiracy and had him put to death on false charges.

The Lord sent Elijah to rebuke Ahab for murdering an innocent man in order to steal his property. Ahab did not stop Jezebel and was responsible before God for Naboth's death. The judgment for this utterly wicked sin would extend to Ahab's entire family line (21-22). Amazingly, at Elijah's rebuke, Ahab was convicted and displayed genuine remorse (27). Because he humbled himself, the Lord showed mercy and promised not to bring judgment in Ahab's own time (29).

The more wicked our sin, or the longer we have persisted in a sin, the harder it is to face it and repent. But no matter what, God is always pleased to show mercy when we repent. In the Lord's work, we can leave behind a good legacy if we stay humble enough to be convicted of sin and repent, even as we get older.

Prayer: Father, thank you that you extend grace to even the most wicked who repent. Help me continually be open to hear your rebuke.

One Word: It's not too late to repent

ONE PROPHET WITH INTEGRITY

1 Kings 22:1-28
Key Verse 22:14

King Ahab invited King Jehoshaphat, a godly king of Judah, to join with him in fighting against the Arameans to take back Ramoth Gilead. Jehoshaphat said they should inquire of the Lord first, but there were not many of the Lord's prophets left in Israel—just false prophets who told Ahab whatever he wanted to hear. Only Micaiah kept his integrity and spoke only what he heard from the Lord (14).

At first Micaiah seemed to also tell the king what he wanted to hear, but he did it in a way that showed he wasn't serious (15b). Maybe Micaiah had a sarcastic streak! When Ahab demanded the truth, Micaiah revealed that it was God's time for Ahab to meet his end for all his sins (20). Ahab's last sin was not listening to the word of the Lord from Micaiah and persecuting him (26-27). Ahab went stubbornly on with his plan.

It is not easy to speak the truth to powerful people when we know it will not please them. Micaiah was one of a very few in Israel who had this integrity. Will I be such a person in my time?

Prayer: Father, help me not be tempted to flatter the powerful but speak with integrity. Please raise up servants of the word like Micaiah in our time.

One Word: Only speak the Lord's words

AHAB'S END

1 Kings 22:29-53
Key Verse 22:38

In defiance of the Lord's word through Micaiah, Ahab king of Israel went up to fight the Arameans at Ramoth Gilead, and Jehoshaphat went with him. In spite of efforts Ahab made to disguise himself (and to expose Jehoshaphat!), he was struck by an arrow shot seemingly at random and died from his wound later the same day. This exactly fulfilled the word of the Lord through Elijah (21:19). Ahab's son ruled in his place, but he was wicked as well (52). Soon the full judgment against Ahab's family would come, as had been prophesied (21:21; Prov 16:4).

Jehoshaphat had been foolish to join the battle after hearing Micaiah's prophecy, but the Lord let him escape with his life (32-33). This was not the only time Jehoshaphat had to learn a lesson to be steered away from greedy pursuits (48).

All plans undertaken apart from the Lord's blessing will fail (Prov 19:21). The only way to obtain a good outcome in our life is to honor the word of the Lord above our selfish desires.

Prayer: Father, thank you that your word proves true without fail. Help me honor your word above earthly success or prosperity.

One Word: God's word is fulfilled

DANIEL'S DECISION OF FAITH

Daniel 1:1-21
Key Verse 1:8

The setting of the book of Daniel is when the Babylonians plundered Judah and carried off the people and their temple treasures to exile in Babylon. Then, the best of Judah's young noblemen were trained for the king's service and in Babylonian literature and language. Among them were Daniel, Hananiah, Mishael and Azariah, who were given new names after the Babylonian gods. As captives, they had no rights and had to submit.

By faith, Daniel resolved not to eat the royal food or drink the royal wine given to them. Daniel's decision required faith to keep his identity as God's holy people and not give in to the pleasure-seeking and idol-worshiping culture. Thus, Daniel boldly asked for permission not to defile himself. God caused the king's chief official to show Daniel favor. But the chief official refused Daniel's request out of fear of the king. It seemed impossible to live a holy life.

Yet Daniel did not give up. By faith he asked his guard to give him and his friends only vegetables and water for ten days and test if they were not healthier. When he made a decision of faith, God blessed them to be healthier and the best of all those being trained. At the end of their 3 years of training, the king himself found none equal to them.

Prayer: Father, please help me to have the courage and wisdom to live a holy life by faith.

One Word: Daniel's decision of faith to be holy

GOD REVEALS TO DANIEL THE KING'S DREAM

Daniel 2:1-30
Key Verse 2:23

The great king of Babylon, Nebuchadnezzar has a disturbing dream that deprives him of any sleep. Though he is very powerful, he is helpless before this dream. In his megalomania, he summons his astrologers and wise men in the middle of the night to tell him his dream and what it means. When they cannot, he orders the execution of all the wisemen in the kingdom, including Daniel and his friends.

When the commander of the guard comes to arrest Daniel, he answers with wisdom and tact. Then, by faith, he boldly goes to the king and asks for time. Though the king refused repeatedly the requests of the other astrologers, he listened to Daniel. It shows that servants who have the spirit of God have spiritual influence and protection. Do you believe this for yourself in your position?

Next, Daniel urged his friends to seek God's mercy in prayer as a life and death matter in an impossible situation. Then, the dream and its meaning were revealed to Daniel. He praises God who has all wisdom and power and is full of light that reveals to his servants the mysteries of his sovereign will and purpose. When we seek his mercy, not only is our problem solved, but we see God's plan in it.

Prayer: Father, please help me to seek your mercy earnestly in prayer and know your wisdom and power. Help me to trust your plan in all things.

One Word: God gives wisdom and power

DANIEL INTERPRETS THE KING'S DREAM

Daniel 2:31-49
Key Verse 2:44

After receiving the meaning of the dream, Daniel immediately goes to the king's guard and halts the execution of the wisemen. When he is brought before the king, he acknowledges that only God in heaven reveals mysteries.

The king's dream was a statue with a head of gold, chest and arms of silver, belly and thighs of bronze, legs of iron, and feet of iron and clay. A rock struck the statue and then became a mountain that filled the earth. The king of Babylon was the head of gold. Other lesser kingdoms would follow. But the rock is Jesus' kingdom which will crush all other kingdoms and will itself endure forever (44). Wherever Christianity went, nations and kingdoms were changed. And Christ's kingdom will never end. Through this dream, Daniel could have hope to persevere by faith in his captivity and wait on the Lord. We can have this hope and be faithful, too.

In awe, King Nebuchadnezzar confessed that Daniel's God is Most High and promoted him. We learn that when he sought God's mercy, Daniel's life was not only spared, but he was lifted up as the king's top official, and his three friends, too. God blesses our faith to seek his mercy.

Prayer: Lord, your kingdom reigns forever. May I live for your kingdom and glory.

One Word: Have hope only in Christ's kingdom which will endure forever

"WE WILL NOT SERVE YOUR GODS"

Daniel 3:1-18
Key Verse 3:18

King Nebuchadnezzar forced his royal officials from greatest to least to bow before a 90-foot image of gold. Otherwise, they would be thrown into a fiery furnace. This is a counterfeit of God's truth in which all those who refuse to bow before Jesus in this life will be thrown into the fiery lake of hell in the next life. The devil works very hard to plant fear of death in our hearts so that we will compromise and bow before false gods and religions. The world gives into these fears, but we Christians must not shrink back in the face of persecution.

Daniel's three friends – Shadrach, Meshach, and Abednego – refused to bow and were brought before the king. He gave them one more chance and planted fear that no god could save them. But they boldly told him that even if they were thrown into the fiery furnace, they trusted that God was more than able to save them (Isaiah 43:2). And even if he chose not to, they trusted God and loved God faithfully and would not serve false gods nor bow before the king's idol. Their faith in God, who is able to save them if he chose, extinguished all the flaming arrows of doubt in the spiritual battle (Eph 6:16). They believed that nothing could separate them from the love of God (Ro 8: 37-38).

Prayer: Father, I repent my fear of persecution and the spirit of compromise. By faith, I trust in your power and love and will serve you only.

One Word: I will serve God only

NO OTHER GOD CAN SAVE

Daniel 3:19-30
Key Verse 3:25

King Nebuchadnezzar's pride was greatly offended by their refusal to bow before his idol. He ordered the fire to be made 7 times hotter and had his strongest soldiers bind them and throw them into the furnace. Ironically, the soldiers were killed by the flames, but Shadrach, Meshach and Abednego were unharmed. Rather, they were walking in the fire – and with them was a fourth man who looked like the Son of God. The king witnessed these things, as did all his officials, and they knew God had saved them. Nebuchadnezzar called to them to come out of the furnace, and they did! God completely saved them! Their story can be our story when we trust in God who loves us and is completely able to save us from every peril (Ps 50:15, 2 Cor 1:10).

In complete fear of God, the king commanded that no one speak a word against God, and the king promoted Shadrach, Meshach, and Abednego. When God's servants refused to bow down to idols or serve other gods, they were saved and prospered. We learn how to live in an anti-Christian world which tries to force us to deny our faith in Christ and abandon godly values and principles.

Prayer: Father, thank you for quenching the fury of the flames (Heb 11:34). Thank you for saving me as no one else can. Help me to stand firm in my faith.

One Word: God alone saves me from the fire

NEBUCHADNEZZAR'S DREAM OF A TREE

Daniel 4:1-18
Key Verse 4:17

This chapter begins with Nebuchadnezzar's proclamation to all the nations about what God has done for him. Though Nebuchadnezzar was the greatest king on earth, he declared that God's kingdom is eternal and God rules over each generation. It was an introduction to his testimony.

While content in his palace, Nebuchadnezzar had another powerful dream. None of his astrologers could interpret it. Finally, Daniel arrived, and the king shared the contents of his dream in which a great tree reached to the sky and extended throughout the earth. It had beautiful leaves and abundant fruit and provided food for all and shelter for the wild animals. Then, a messenger from heaven came down, pronounced judgment on the tree, it was cut down, and its stump chained. Next, the angel pronounced judgment on a man that he would be drenched with dew, eat plants, and have the mind of an animal for 7 years. The angel announced that through this judgment, all people would know that God is Most High, and he sets over the nations of the world anyone he chooses. This is a strong reminder to stay humble and give glory to God. Power corrupts and makes us unnecessarily proud. We desperately need humility to honor God as Lord Most High.

Prayer: Father, you are sovereign over leaders and nations – and me. Help me to humble myself completely under Jesus as Lord Most High.

One Word: God is Most High over all the earth

RENOUNCE YOUR SINS

Daniel 4:19-27
Key Verse 4:27

Daniel was distressed about telling the king the bad news and tactfully said how he wished that the dream applied to Nebuchadnezzar's enemies. Then, Daniel explained that the amazing tree in the dream applied to the king and his empire. He was the greatest on earth. But he would be cut down, live with the animals eating grass, and not restored until he confessed that God in Heaven is Most High. This nightmare would be Nebuchadnezzar's future unless he accepted Daniel's advice to renounce his sins and be kind to the oppressed. His empire reached to the ends of the earth. He had great authority to bring about justice to the poor and weak. But as long as he clung to his sins, he would blind himself to injustice and be found guilty by God. So, God gave Nebuchadnezzar this dream and Daniel as his adviser to give him an opportunity to repent and use his vast power for good.

We are easily the same. Success deprives us of the ability to keenly see our own weaknesses, especially our arrogant pride, indifference, loss of perspective, and powerlessness to do what is right. Let's also hear God's word to renounce our sins!

Prayer: Father, thank you for warning me to repent. Help me to hear your words today and humble myself. Grant me your Holy Spirit to repent and do what is right (Jn 16:8).

One Word: Renounce your sins

NEBUCHADNEZZAR IS HUMBLED

Daniel 4:28-37
Key Verse 4:37

When Nebuchadnezzar saw his royal city Babylon, he praised his own glory, majesty, and power. Then, judgment was pronounced from heaven, and he was stripped of all his glory. He became insane and lived among the wild animals eating grass for 7 years. The emperor resembled an eagle with his long, white, unkempt hair and beard cascading down and unclipped nails. Finally, he looked up to heaven and surrendered to God. His sanity was restored, and he praised God and gave glory to him.

Nebuchadnezzar acknowledged that God does what he pleases, and no one can stop his hand or question his authority. Then, his nobles sought him out and restored him to his throne, and he was greater than before. But he learned his lesson to only praise and exalt God who does what is right. He also learned that God humbles the proud. What a hard way to learn!

Let's be humble and praise God when we see our own version of Babylon. May we guard our lips and hearts to praise only Jesus for his love and his righteousness and devote ourselves to do good (He 13:15,16).

Prayer: Father, please forgive my proud lips and help me to exalt you only.

One Word: God humbles the proud and raises up the humble

THE WRITING ON THE WALL

Daniel 5:1-21
Key Verse 5:20

Sometime later, King Belshazzar, a descendant of Nebuchadnezzar, ruled the empire. At his party for 1,000 nobles and their wives and concubines, they drank from the gold and silver goblets from the temple in Jerusalem and praised other gods. Then, a hand appeared and wrote on the plaster of the wall near the lampstand so they could all see. The king was terrified, and his knees shook. He called for the wisemen and offered great rewards. But no one could solve it. Then, the queen mother came into the hall and urged the king to call for Daniel.

Daniel reminded the king of Nebuchadnezzar's story. In his generation, God raised him up to be the greatest. But when he became arrogant, God humbled him and made him like an animal until he confessed that God is Most High, and he sets over kingdoms anyone he wants. We learn how important it is to teach the next generation about God Most High – to worship him and to acknowledge him as Sovereign Lord, who humbles the proud and raises up the humble.

Prayer: Lord, please help me to have a sense of history and to honor God as Most High. Help my children to worship you and be humble.

One Word: Humbly fear God and worship him

HONOR GOD WHO HOLDS YOUR LIFE

Daniel 5:22-31
Key Verse 5:23

King Belshazzar knew all about God's work in King Nebuchadnezzar's life. But Belshazzar chose not to humble himself. Rather, he chose to rebel against God, he chose a life of depravity and debauchery, and he chose to praise other gods. He failed to acknowledge that God holds in his hands his life and his ways. Tragically, many people know all about God and the Bible, but they harden their hearts and choose to rebel against God. They want to be the center of their own world.

Daniel read the inscription on the wall that predicted God's judgment of King Belshazzar. God graciously warned him before it was too late. Though he heard God's word very clearly and the great servant of God Daniel counseled him, he chose not to repent. That very night, it all came true. Belshazzar was killed, and his empire was taken over by the Medes and Persians. Likewise, God's warning in the Bible is clear. God will repay each person according to what he deserves (Ro 2:5-10). May we persist in doing good and seek his glory, honor, and immortality. May we also guide the wayward ones to repent and honor God before it is too late and help them to the end.

Prayer: Lord, please help me to honor you with my life and in all my ways. May I shepherd to the end those who have rebelled against you.

One Word: Honor God who holds in his hands my life and all my ways

DANIEL'S LIFE OF PRAYER

Daniel 6:1-15
Key Verse 6:10

The new king Darius appointed Daniel as one of his top administrators. And because Daniel was trustworthy, the king wanted to put Daniel over all his empire. Out of jealousy, other magistrates plotted against Daniel and tried to trap him by persecuting him for his faith. They tricked the king into decreeing that everyone must pray only to him for the next 30 days. Anyone who violated the king's order would be thrown into the lion's den.

When Daniel learned of the law, he went home to his upstairs room and with his windows open, he got down on his knees and prayed, giving thanks to God just as he had done before. Daniel did not hide his faith. But he came to the Lord praying and thanking him (Ph 4:6-7). He did not live a double life based on the situation to save himself.

Daniel's enemies caught him praying to God for help and reported him to the King. Though the king wanted to protect Daniel, they put pressure on Darius to keep the law. Likewise, we face high pressure situations where our faith in Jesus gets us in jeopardy. The persecution is real, and there is no one who can save us. We must faithfully pray to God and ask for his help (Is 41:10). We must not be afraid, but trust in God's love. (1 Jn 4:18)

Prayer: Father, please strengthen me to pray to you in the face of persecution and seek your help.

One Word: Faithfully pray and seek God's help

DANIEL IN THE LION'S DEN

Daniel 6:16-28
Key Verse 6:27

King Darius was pressured by wicked men to throw Daniel in the lion's den. The king himself expressed his hope that God would save Daniel. After a sleepless night, King Darius rushed to the den and asked Daniel if God had saved him. Daniel testified that God's angel shut the lions' mouths because he was innocent. When they pulled him out, there was no wound on him because he trusted in God. Then, the king commanded the other satraps who falsely accused Daniel be thrown in the lions' den, along with their families. They symbolized the end of all liars who persecute the people of God. The king made a new law that everyone in his kingdom must fear God. He proclaimed that God's kingdom will never end, and he rescues and saves those who fear him as he rescued Daniel from the lions. Then, Daniel prospered in his reign and Cyrus' reign.

Like Daniel, we suffer much when we are attacked for our faith and are falsely accused. It is the best time to pray, thank God, and trust in his help. Prayer is our spiritual weapon. When no one can help us, God can. (Ps 143:8,9) In all things, his purpose is to reveal his glory on earth that he is the living God who saves and rescues those who trust in him.

Prayer: Father, forgive my fears. Help me to pray faithfully, thank you, and rely on your help.

One Word: Pray to God who rescues and saves

AN EVERLASTING KINGDOM

Daniel 7:1-28
Key Verse 7:27

During the first year of Belshazzar's reign, Daniel had a vision of 4 beasts: a lion, a bear, a leopard, and a very terrifying and frightening beast. These beasts had authority to rule for a while and affected the world of their times. They are powerful and boastful. But the Ancient of Days will take his seat, and he will judge them. The Son of Man will receive from the Ancient of Days all authority, glory and sovereign power. All nations and peoples of every language will worship him. His kingdom will never end. Though wicked people oppress God's people and slander God, in the end, they will be destroyed forever. And the sovereignty, greatness, and power of all the kingdoms of the world will be handed over to the holy people of God Most High. His kingdom will be an everlasting kingdom.

Often, we are suffering greatly from the darkness of evil systems, and we are wondering what is going on in this world? In the end, Christ will come, his kingdom will endure forever, and we will be co-heirs with Christ. We must patiently endure and keep our hope in heaven above (2 Ti 2:11-12).

Prayer: Father, thank you for giving us real hope to reign forever with you in your everlasting kingdom. Please help me to persevere in doing your will.

One Word: Have hope to reign with Christ in God's eternal kingdom

A VISION OF A RAM AND A GOAT

Daniel 8:1-27
Key Verse 8:17

Again during Belshazzar's reign, Daniel had another vision. This time he saw a ram that was very powerful and conquered the north, west, and south, and did whatever it pleased. Next, he saw a goat who came from the west and attacked the ram furiously and trampled on him. The goat became very great, but at the height of his power, his horn was broken off. Then, 4 other horns grew in his place. One of them grew powerful and oppressed the Beautiful Land and God's people. Then, the daily sacrifices were stopped, and the sanctuary was brought low. This wicked ruler prospered, and truth was thrown to the ground.

An angel explained to Daniel that these things regarded the end times. The vision of the ram was about Media and Persia; the vision of the goat was Greece. The 4 horns represented 4 kingdoms that emerged from his empire. A wicked king will rise up and oppress God's holy people. Later, God will bring him to an end, too.

The world is so dark that God's people can lose their vision. We need to affirm that God is in control. Kingdoms rise and fall. His judgment will come. In all kinds of tribulations, we must faithfully trust in God and be patient in hope with his vision.

Prayer: Father, thank you for giving us your vision that the end of this world will come. Help us to patiently have hope in you and be faithful to you.

One Word: Have God's vision and be patient

DANIEL'S PRAYER

Daniel 9:1-27
Key Verse 9:18

In the first year of Darius, Daniel realized from Scripture that God's destruction of Jerusalem would last 70 years. Then, he humbly pleaded with God in prayer, put on sackcloth and ashes, and fasted. He praised God for his faithfulness in keeping his promises to those who love him and obeyed his commands. He confessed the sins of his people and repented for their rebellion, their disobedience, and their refusal to listen to God's prophets. And he pleaded for God's mercy not because of anything they have done, but because of his great Name. He asked for God's mercy and favor to restore his holy city and people who bear his Name. While he was praying, the angel Gabriel came and told him the holy city would take years to restore, the Anointed One would die there, the city would be destroyed, and war would never end. Jerusalem could not be their hope, but God's everlasting kingdom is their living hope (1 Pet 1:3,4).

As Christians, may we humbly fast and pray for people of all nations to seek God's forgiveness, mercy, and glory. We are sinful and rebellious and deserve God's judgment. But may God have mercy on us not because of anything we have done, but so that his Name might be glorified and proclaimed in the earth through us (Jn 17:20).

Prayer: Father, please help me to pray for all nations to receive your mercy through Jesus.

One Word: Pray for God's mercy on all people

DANIEL RECEIVES A REVELATION

Daniel 10:1-11:1
Key Verse 10:12

In the third year of Cyrus, king of Persia, Daniel received a revelation of a great war. It greatly troubled him. He ate no choice food nor meat or wine. He then had a vision of a heavenly man who was dressed in white linen and a golden belt, who had a golden body and a face like lightning, and who no one else could see. Gazing at him, Daniel was so weak, he turned deathly pale and was helpless. Then he heard the heavenly man speak to him, and he fell into a deep sleep. The heavenly man touched him, strengthened him, and told him to listen carefully. He explained that as soon as Daniel humbled himself through fasting and prayer to gain wisdom and understanding, his words were heard and the heavenly man was sent to help him, but he was detained in a spiritual battle with the prince of Persia. Hearing this, Daniel was speechless and could barely breathe. The heavenly man touched him again and gave Daniel peace and strength to hear his explanation of the vision of the great war.

From this, we learn that we need to fast and pray to have God's wisdom and understanding. It is hard to fight the spiritual battle, and it drains us. But God will help us and strengthen us with his peace and spiritual power until we know his will.

Prayer: Father, help me to humble myself to fight the spiritual battle through prayer and fasting and receive your wisdom and strength.

One Word: Humbly fast and pray like Daniel

THE KINGS OF THIS WORLD

Daniel 11:2-27
Key Verse 11:27

The heavenly man explained that the Persian Empire will have 4 more kings and will fight against Greece. Then, a mighty king will come next who will do as he pleases. After him, his kingdom will be parceled out toward the four winds. A kingdom will form in the South towards Egypt and the Beautiful Land, and another kingdom will be in the North by Syria. These two kingdoms will fight back and forth for years, plundering, killing thousands in battle, and bringing devastation to the Beautiful Land, which was caught in between. God's people would suffer from various kinds of oppression. Some Hebrew men would rebel, but they would fail. The war would continue for a long time, there would be intrigue, enemies within and without, and no lasting peace. Two kings would sit at a table bent on evil and lie to each other, but to no avail because God would appoint a time to end.

This vision teaches us that God is sovereign over wars, conspiracies, and oppression. All these forces of darkness will come to an end at his appointed time. His people must be faithful, be patient, and put their hope in his kingdom. We must trust in his sovereignty (Col 1:16,17).

Prayer: Father, please help me to be patient. Help me to see you are in control and will end wars in your right time.

One Word: Be patient for God's appointed time

THE TIME OF THE END WILL COME

Daniel 11:28-45
Key Verse 11:35

The heavenly man continues to explain how the king of the North will set his heart against the holy covenant of God and will persecute God's people. The war will turn into a religious genocide as he tries to force people to abandon their faith, reward people who do, and vent his fury at those who don't. He will desecrate the temple and abolish the daily sacrifice. He will set up the abomination that causes desolation in the temple. He will corrupt God's people. But those who know God will firmly resist him. Those who are wise will instruct many, though they are killed by the sword, burned, and captured. Sincere people will help them. Some of the wise will stumble, so that they may be refined, purified, and made spotless until the end, which will come at God's appointed time. Next, there will arise another king who will magnify himself, defy God, set up his own god, and cause a great war in the Holy Land. Then, he, too, will come to his end.

In our lives, trials and tribulations will come. We must be wise and instruct others in the faith. When we fail, God is faithful to refine us, purify us, and make us spotless (Phil 2:15, 1 Peter 1:6,7). We must faithfully serve God, put our hope in him, and patiently trust in his sovereignty.

Prayer: Father, please help me to be wise, to serve you faithfully, and put my hope in you.

One Word: Be purified and made spotless

THE WISE WILL SHINE LIKE THE STARS

Daniel 12:1-13
Key Verse 12:3

The heavenly man concludes that there will be a time of great distress as never has happened before, and God will protect his people. Those whose names are written in the book of life will be delivered. Multitudes will rise from dead: some to eternal life and some to everlasting punishment. Those who are wise and instructed others in righteousness will shine like the stars forever and ever. Then, the scroll was closed. Daniel saw two more heavenly men had joined them, and one asked about the time when these events would happen. The heavenly man said that when the power of the holy people has been finally broken, the end will come. Daniel longed to know more. But the heavenly man told him to go his way. The scroll was closed. He remarked that many will be purified and made spotless, and the wicked will continue to be wicked. Blessed is the one who patiently waits and puts their hope in God until the end.

We wonder about the end times, and God gives us here a vision about it to help us live wisely and have hope. We must be patient through all kinds of evil events and put our hope in God's everlasting kingdom. Then, our hearts will be purified and spotless, and we can shine like the stars forever!

Prayer: Father, please help me to live wisely and put my hope in your kingdom.

One Word: Be wise and lead many to righteousness

INTRODUCTION TO HAGGAI

Haggai wrote around 520 B.C., in the time following the return of the first exiles to Jerusalem. They returned to rebuild the temple of the Lord, and they had laid the foundation, but when they met resistance from the local people, they became frightened and stopped the project, reasoning that the time had not yet come to rebuild the temple. As time passed, they took care to rebuild their own comfortable homes, families, and lives, but the temple remained in ruins. Haggai then encouraged these people to overcome their fear. "This is what I covenanted with you when you came out of Egypt. And my Spirit remains among you. Do not fear!" (2:5) The people listened to Haggai, and the temple was finished around 515 B.C.

GIVE CAREFUL THOUGHT TO YOUR WAYS

Haggai 1:1-15
Key Verse 1:5

After 70 years of exile in Babylon, the people of Israel, according to the word of the Lord, were allowed to go back to their homeland and rebuild the temple of the Lord their God. Work began in earnest, but it quickly came to a halt when opposition to the building came up. They reasoned that it must not be the right time to build the house of the Lord. Then the word of the Lord came to the prophet Haggai to Zerubbabel, governor of Judah and Joshua the high priest. The Lord rebuked them for living in comfort in their paneled houses, while the temple of the Lord remained in ruins. He told them twice to give careful thought to their ways. Their struggles were from the Lord, that they may repent and come back to him and build his house.

When they heard the word of the Lord, Zerubbabel and Joshua repented their ways, along with the whole remnant in Judah, and they began building the house of the Lord. Life has many struggles that keep us very busy. It is easy to forget the Lord amidst those struggles. But let us give careful thought to our ways and come back to him.

Prayer: Father, help me to repent my busyness and lack of thought to your ways. Help me to think carefully about my ways and deeply consider yours.

One Word. Give careful thought to your ways

GOD DESIRES MORE THAN A BUILDING

Haggai 2:1-23
Key Verse 2:7

When the original, glorious temple was built in the days of King Solomon, the whole nation was involved. Even nations outside of Judah participated in the construction of the temple by bringing cut timber to be used in the building. But the building of the temple at the time of the returned remnant was to be done by a very few people. When they repented at Haggai's word and started again to build the temple, they were discouraged because it looked so pitiful. There was no way, they thought, it would ever compare to the glory of the original temple. But the Lord taught them it is not outside appearance that is important. What mattered was that the glory of the Lord imbibed the temple. The temple was more than gold and silver; it was the sign that the Lord's Presence was with them.

According to the Law, they were defiled because of sin. Yet the Lord from that day on, would come to them and bless them. He would consecrate them and purify them.

Prayer: Father, you are glorious God. May your glory fill the temple of our hearts each and every moment. Come to us, cleanse us, and bless us.

One Word: Seek God's glory

INTRODUCTION TO OBADIAH

Obadiah means "servant of the Lord" or "worshipper of the Lord". He was from Judah and was called to tell of God's judgment against the nation of Edom. Two accepted dates for this prophecy are between 941 BC and 853 BC when King Jehoram and Jerusalem were attacked by the Philistine/Arab coalition (2Chron 21:16) or 586 BC when Jerusalem was destroyed by the Babylonians (2Kings 25:2; 2Chron 25:36).

Obadiah is the shortest book in the Old Testament. Obadiah is written in the form of a poetic dirge. Because of their treachery and pride, Edom stood condemned and would be destroyed. The prophecy shows that God judges those who have harmed his people and responds towards anyone who harms his children. It also tells of God's desire for his kingdom to spread throughout the land. God wants his people to experience deliverance and the peace of the Kingdom of God. There are two mega themes in the book: justice and pride.

DELIVERANCE ON MOUNT ZION

Obadiah 1:1-21
Key Verse 21

The nation of Edom had common ancestry with the nations of Israel and Judah. Edom was descended from Jacob's brother Esau. The nations should have been close allies. But Edom had become proud and boastful. They believed their nation was impervious to attack from outside. Many in the cities of Petra and Sela lived in cliffside dwellings, making conquering the nation very difficult. They became complacent, proud, arrogant, and boastful. When their sister nation Judah experienced hardship, they gloated. They helped themselves to her spoils. Although these things happened to Judah because of judgment on her sin, the Lord would punish Edom for her sins as well. Edom would be destroyed.

God would bring about a reversal of fortune for both Judah and Edom. He would restore his people, while Edom would become like stubble that gets completely consumed in the fire. Deliverers would govern the mountains of Esau. The kingdom of Edom would be the Lord's.

Prayer: Father, those who are proud and boastful, you bring down to the ground. Help me to repent that I may dwell in your presence.

One Word: The kingdom is the Lord's

March

Sun	Mon	Tue	Wed	Thu	Fri	Sat
23	24	25	26	27	28	1
2	3	4	5	6	7	8
9	10	11	12	13	14	15
16	17	18	19	20	21	22
23	24	25	26	27	28	29
30	31	1	2	3	4	5

ABRAM GROWS TO TRUST GOD MORE

Genesis 12:10-13:18
Key Verse 13:17

When there was a severe famine in the land, Abram made a reasonable decision to move to Egypt. He also prompted his beautiful wife Sarai to lie about their relationship so that he could gain favor with Pharaoh. His sense of responsibility for his household's well-being and security became a stumbling block, causing him to forget the presence of God in his life and lead others to sin.

God was gracious even as Abram failed to trust him and intervened to save him from Pharaoh's rage. When Abram returned to the promised land, Abram became prosperous. However, the blessing brought a different problem. The land could not support the growing livestock of both Abram and his nephew Lot, and their workers often quarreled. Learning his lessons from God's provision, Abram took the high road in resolving the problem, letting Lot choose where he wanted to stay and let him go.

Abram's action was a step forward in his life of faith. God encouraged Abram by taking him on a walk around the land and assured him of His promises. Abram might have lost the better part of the land and his nephew Lot as a companion. But he had God as his reward.

Prayer: Father, you are my provider and comforter. I fear no one as I hold to your promises. I am not afraid to be lonely, as you are on my side.

One Word: Trust God and find peace and comfort.

ABRAM'S VICTORY

Genesis 14:1-24
Key Verse 14:19,20

During a conflict among Canaanite kings, Abram's nephew Lot, who lived in Sodom (13:10,11), was captured as a prisoner of war. The circumstances brought Abram into the war, as he desired to rescue his nephew.

Upon hearing about Lot's captivity, Abram gathered 318 trained men from his household to begin his pursuit. He strategically attacked the party that kept Lot and succeeded in recovering him, Lot's people, and all of Lot's possessions. In response, Lot returned to his home in Sodom, attracting the attention of the king of Sodom, who visited Abram.

God sent his messenger Melchizedek to encourage Abram at that time. Through Melchizedek's blessing, Abram was reminded of God's presence in his life and that God himself led him to win against the kings. With this assurance, he was not intimidated when he met the king of Sodom and refused his offer of material gains. He knew that blessings came from God and trusted that God would give him abundantly according to his promise. Do you feel tired and burdened negotiating the affairs of the world? Bring your trust before our almighty God, who encourages and brings us victory.

Prayer: Father, all things belong to you. Please help me fight a spiritual battle each day to overcome all human thinking and trust you fully.

One Word: Victory belongs to God.

ABRAM WAS CALLED RIGHTEOUS BY FAITH

Genesis 15:1-21
Key Verse 15:6

Knowing Abram's heart, God himself came to him to encourage him. God told him not to be afraid: God was Abram's shield and reward. By rescuing Lot and defeating the local kings, Abram had entered dangerous political waters and only stood to lose, humanly speaking. But as God addressed Abram's larger problem, fear, Abram revealed his profound frustration—he still had no child to pass on his blessings. His calculations of who might be his heir only brought him to further depression.

God affirmed his promise to make Abram a father, and no one other than his biological child would be his heir. And Abram believed those words. There was no tangible change, but Abram believed the promise because he believed in God. And his faith made him righteous before God.

God ratified his covenant with Abram through a customary ritual, a covenant of one-sided grace. God alone bore the burden of commitment to fulfill his promise and assured Abram. Do you struggle with unbelief because of human circumstances? Believe in our gracious and faithful God, who possesses heaven and the earth and guarantees our inheritance (Eph 1:13).

Prayer: Father, you are in control, and everything belongs to you. Please help me hear your voice and receive the assurance of your promises. I believe in your promises because I believe in you.

One Word: Abram believed the Lord

HAGAR HAD SEEN GOD, WHO SEES HER

Genesis 16:1-16
Key Verse 16:13

Sarai's reasonable advice caused Abram's next stumble. Sarai suggested that Abram sleep with her slave so that he could have a child. Abram probably knew the advice did not align with God's promise of the rightful heir, but he chose to listen to his wife.

The slave Hagar became pregnant, which brought trouble to their house. Hagar became proud, and Sarai blamed Abram. In reply, Abram avoided his responsibility as the head of the family and let Sarai handle the problem. So, Sarai drove the girl into misery, and she fled, carrying Abram's child. Amid self-created problems with no good solutions, God intervened.

He sent his messenger to Hagar, assured her of her child's birth and safety, and told her to return and submit to her mistress. The prophecy about her child and God's direction to her may challenge our modern sensibilities. However, Hagar believed: the sovereign God was always watching over her. She was moved. While Sarai and Abram had no respect or concern for her, God did not ignore her, a slave, and guided her to do what was right with an assurance of protection. Today, would you also come to God, who sees you? He will guide you as he knows you and cares about you.

Prayer: Father, I bring my weariness before you. I trust you to guide me in your perfect plans.

One Word: God sees me

THE SIGN OF GOD'S COVENANT

Genesis 17:1-27
Key Verse 17:1,2

There is a 13-year gap between chapters 16 and 17. Now, Abram is 99 years old, content with his life as Ishmael's father (18). Once, Abram had faith that pleased God (15:6). However, he failed to hold the covenant God had given him: to trust in God's promise of blessings. Instead, he lived according to the customs of his generation by having a child from a slave girl.

Abram might have forgotten about the covenant, but God did not. God appeared to him after Abram's long break. Changes in circumstances and the passing of time did not change who God was and what he had promised. In one year, God would give Abram a son from Sarai, the true heir of God's blessings. Until then, Abram must uphold his part of the covenant: have faith in God.

To help Abram remember God's covenant, God changed Abram's name to Abraham and Sarai to Sarah. Also, as a sign, Abraham and all males in his household would undergo circumcision. Even though Abraham's faith weakened, God, with his almighty power, still planned to raise Abraham as a father of many nations.

Prayer: Father, you gave me a covenant with one- sided grace. Thank you for faithfully holding onto me so that I would grow to understand your will and participate in your work.

One Word: The faithfulness of God leads me

"SARAH WILL HAVE A SON"

Genesis 18:1-15
Key Verse 18:14

After Abraham's household had been circumcised (17:26-27), God visited again in the form of three men (2). In the heat of the day, Abraham, even at a hundred years old, hurried to welcome them (2-5), hurried and ran to served food (6-8a), and waited on them (8b). What gave him such vigor? It seems the promise of God regarding the birth of Isaac reverberated in Abraham's heart, filling him with joy and spirit. Faith in God's promise renewed his strength like a soaring eagle (Isa 40:31). Joyful faith is the secret of youth.

God had not come only to visit Abraham, but to address Sarah (9). Abraham had heard it before (17:19), but Sarah seemed to be struggling, even laughing at the announcement (12), just as Abraham had done (17:17). It was not a laugh of joy, but to cover a lifetime of pain, shame, and longing. God understood Sarah, and gave her one word to hold on to: "Is anything too hard for the LORD?" God would turn her embarrassing laugh into an endless source of joy for them at the birth of Isaac, whose name means laughter. In the same way, God understands each of us, and sent his Son Jesus to us to address the inner reality of our heart. We need only trust him and his promise and experience the joy of faith today.

Prayer: Father, thank you for healing my deep wounds and longings through Jesus. Help me to trust you today and experience the joy of faith.

One Word: Jesus came to heal our wounded hearts

KEEP THE WAY OF THE LORD

Genesis 18:16-33
Key Verse 18:19

God was about to deal with Sodom, whose evil had been ongoing for a long time (13:13). God had a clear plan, but he included his friend Abraham in this. Why? God had chosen Abraham to be a great nation through whom all the earth would be blessed. But it would require directing his children and household to keep the ways of the LORD. God saw the situation with Sodom – and Abraham's nephew Lot – as a time of revealing Abraham's mind and heart. How would Abraham respond?

Hearing about God's plan to visit Sodom (20-21), Abraham took it upon himself to plead for the righteous people in Sodom – not on the basis of their righteousness or his influence with God, but on the basis of God's good and just character (25). It was hard for Abraham, who feared God, to continue to press the number down to ten, but he did so, and each time God fully agreed with Abraham's request, even to spare the city for the sake of ten. In this way, Abraham demonstrated "keeping the way of the LORD by doing what is just and right," as a good shepherd for his nephew. Jesus tells us our days are just like the days of Lot (Lk 17:28). We learn from Abraham how to model the way of the LORD in our times through crying out in mercy for sinners Jesus came to save.

Prayer: Father, thank you for your great mercy on me and my family. In days like these, help me cry out in prayer for even one lost soul today.

One Word: Justice tempered with mercy

"THE LORD WAS MERCIFUL TO THEM"

Genesis 19:1-38
Key Verse 19:16

Lot's choice of compromise and comfort in Sodom bore bad fruit (13:10-13). The angels sent to Sodom are not enamored with Lot's "hospitality." The townsfolk, whom Lot considered his "friends" (7), were violently evil (4-5), and did not respect him (9). Nor did his own sons-in-law (14). Even when being saved, he could not really trust God, seeking comfort in Zoar (20-22). His compromise damaged his family: his wife looked back and became a pillar of salt (26). Jesus says it is a warning against being entrapped by the things of this world (Lk 17:30-32). Lot's daughters had not learned the way of God like Abraham's family (18:19), but rather learned to follow what was "the custom all over the earth" (31), leading to the origin of two enemy tribes: the Moabites and the Ammonites.

In spite of all this, God was merciful to Lot and his family (16), and delivered them, remembering Abraham his friend (29). Lot's story is a lesson to wholeheartedly pursue God, as the consequences are too terrible – not only for us, but our family and society as well. But it is also a lesson of our God's great mercy. Let's respond to his mercy and pray for our people to do so as well.

Prayer: Father, you are so merciful to me, even when I'm stubborn like Lot. Help me to trust in your mercy and seek your ways each day. Hear our prayer for the people around us to trust you too.

One Word: God's mercy is revealed in Jesus

GOD RESCUES SARAH IN GERAR

Genesis 20:1-18
Key Verse 20:3

After seeing the devastation of Sodom (19:27-28), Abraham retreats into Gerar, and is once again overcome with fear enough to trade his wife for his security (2, 11-13). There is a saying, "Never meet your heroes," because we find they are full of weaknesses just like we are.

Verse 3 begins with powerful words: "But God..." God is not intimidated, discouraged, or frustrated. God rises to the moment and confronts Abimelek, defends Sarah, while fully supporting Abraham (3- 7). God's arm is not too short to save; where we may grow weak and fail, our God is faithful and mighty! In the ensuing confrontation, Abraham makes weak excuses, while Abimelek is very conciliatory (8-15). He respects Abraham, opening his land to him, and believes God's words regarding Abraham's prayer. He also directly addresses Sarah, restoring her dignity (16). Finally, Abraham prays for Abimelek's household, and the curse is lifted (17-18).

Behind all this, we see God shepherd the covenant family, particularly Sarah. By closing and opening the wombs of the entire populace for her, it touches her lifelong wound of barrenness, planting faith again that nothing is too hard for God (18:14).

Prayer: Father, as you rescued Sarah, you have rescued us through Jesus' cross. Help me trust in you and learn your faithfulness today.

One Word: We are weak but he is strong

"LAUGHTER" IS BORN TO SARAH

Genesis 21:1-21
Key Verse 21:1

Both Abraham (17:17) and Sarah (18:12) had laughed at the impossibility of having a son. One year later "the LORD was gracious to Sarah ... and ...did for Sarah what he had promised." They could finally understand God's joy in naming him Isaac (17:19). Sarah saw this as a source of joy for everyone, not only her. Her crushed spirit was restored. God's promises fulfilled through Jesus reveal his faithfulness and are a source of joy to us.

Hagar's teenage son did not laugh but mocked. Abraham and Sarah's sin against Hagar continued to hurt the family. But God intervened, affirming Isaac while directing Hagar and Ishmael to be sent out. Sending them away was the painful cost of sin, which God took responsibility for on their behalf.

Hagar's life has been hard as an abused slave, used up and then cast aside. But God did not abandon her. God visits her again, calls her by name, provides words of comfort and direction, and opens her eyes to his providence for them. God's mindfulness for her and her son reminds us of our Lord Jesus, who came to seek and to save the lost (Lk 19:10). Sometimes we or our loved ones feel like Hagar sobbing in the desert, needing God's intervention. Let's pray to our merciful God.

Prayer: Father, remind me of the joy of salvation that I may laugh today. Please intervene in the lives of today's Hagar and Ishmael.

One Word: God keeps his promises

ABRAHAM CALLED ON THE ETERNAL GOD

Genesis 21:22-34
Key Verse 21:33

The last time Abraham encountered Abimelek he had been full of fear, cowardly gave up his wife, and made weak excuses (20:1-18). God had intervened at that time. Abimelek feared God. He kept his eye on Abraham, and saw that God was with him in everything. So he sought out a treaty of mutual respect. The world is watching how we live. Do they see that God is with us in everything?

Abraham is a different man. His fear has been replaced with courage. He not only agrees to the treaty, but even confronts Abimelek about a well he dug ("complained" is better translated "reprove" or "rebuke"). With confidence and faith in God who makes and keeps promises, Abraham became bold and courageous.

The introduction of the term "Philistines" here reminds us that we live in hostile territory. Abraham doesn't fight his neighbors but makes friends and allies. His planting a tamarisk tree and calling out to the Eternal God shows where his strength comes from. He does not retreat but stays a long time. Beersheba becomes a prominent place in God's history from this time forward.

Prayer: Father, you have been so faithful. Open my eyes to know you as the Eternal God, that your perfect love may drive out all my fear. Help me be a peacemaker in a world of fear and conflict.

One Word: Our God is the Eternal God

GOD TELLS ABRAHAM TO SACRIFICE ISAAC

Genesis 22:1-24
Key Verse 22:2

Such a command is unthinkable – a reverting of God's promise. The test for Abraham was to trust God with not only his own life, but with his son – his only son – whom he loves. This is the first time the word love appears in the Bible. Abraham's love for Isaac is a foreshadow of God's love for his Son Jesus (Mt 3:17), whom he sacrificed for us. Silently preparing, taking the journey, engaging with Isaac as they ascend the mountain, even to the point of binding the boy and wielding the knife – all of it tested Abraham's confidence in God who would "provide;" Abraham's faith was justified.

The name Moriah means region of seeing. In a play on words, Abraham calls the place "YHWH sees to it," or "the LORD Provides." It meant more than he could imagine. The ram provided atonement for Isaac; the temple built here centuries later provided atonement for Israel (2Ch 3:1). But the temple points to Jesus (Jn 2:19-21), and his atoning sacrifice opened the way of salvation for all people. The LORD Provides indeed!

God tested Abraham because he wanted to transfer the covenant from being conditionally based on Abraham's obedience (12:1-3) to an unconditional covenant based on God alone (16).

Prayer. Father, you have provided everything in Jesus. Help me to trust you with all that I love.

One Word: The New Covenant is unconditional

ABRAHAM BURIES SARAH AT HEBRON

Genesis 23:1-20
Key Verse 23:19

Sarah had 37 years of domestic life together with Abraham and Isaac, and then died in Hebron. She is the only woman in the Bible whose lifespan was recorded, another sign of her importance. God valued Sarah, cared for her so intimately, and took her to himself, but her example lives on in our faith.

Abraham was in mourning. But Sarah's burial needed to be handled. Abraham had to engage thoroughly, contextually, humbly with his neighbors to purchase the burial plot for his dead wife Sarah. Although a "foreigner," he is very competent and understands the procedures of engaging in such a transaction. On their part, the Hittites treat him with great respect, not only as an equal, but a "prince among us." He earned that respect through his humility (7), cultural sensitivity and contextual awareness. Hebron means "unity" as with friends. Abraham spent money to make an alliance with the Hittites. Jesus tells us to use wealth to make friends (Lk 16:9). To do so we need to learn humility.

With this deal complete, Abraham finally has legal rights to the land, a foothold upon which God would build a tribe, a nation, a kingdom through him. The daily things of our lives also have great potential, as the kingdom grows through these (Mt 13:31-32).

Prayer: Father, your care for Sarah moves my heart to trust you more. Help me learn Abraham's humility in all things today, trusting your purposes.

One Word: Sarah was buried like a seed in Canaan

GOD WILL PROVIDE A WIFE FOR ISAAC

Genesis 24:1-9
Key Verse 24:7

After a life full of blessing, Abraham focuses his attention on Isaac, who is at least thirty-seven (17:17; 23:1) yet still unmarried, likely due to his mom's death (24:67). Being too old to journey back to his brother Nahor's family, Abraham charges his servant under oath to get a wife for his son. The servant realizes the difficulty of the task, "What if she is unwilling to come?" Abraham's focus is "Do not bring him back there!" Instead, holding again to God's promise and faithfulness, Abraham puts his trust in God who will provide a way to bring a wife.

Abraham's assigned task from God was to teach his children the way of the LORD (18:19), and this included marriage. We too pray for our own marriages, those of our children and grandchildren – that we may see God's vision to lavish love on a thousand generations of those who love him and keep his covenant. Let's pray and trust God.

Additionally, we see the trusting friendship between Abraham and his servant. He shared his heart, the servant responded with concerns, and this sensitive and intimate matter was discussed frankly. The servant pledges himself to it. Do we have such people in our community? Are we such people? Our future depends on this.

Prayer: Father, we cry out to you to provide for faithful and holy families to be established, particularly among the coming generations.

One Word: Trust God and marry by faith

"PRAISE BE TO THE LORD WHO HAS LED ME"

Genesis 24:10-49
Key Verse 24:26-27

To find a wife for Isaac in a faraway land required strategy to "feel out" God's faithfulness to Abraham, ultimately identifying Rebekah. Location is important so he went to Nahor, not waiting for her to show up. Standard is important; not beauty or purity, which Rebekah has both of, but hospitality, service and kindness, which she demonstrated (18- 20). But most importantly, the servant sought God's clear direction in this (21), even to the point of refusing dinner (33) until the answer was clear (49).

Seeing God's hand at work, the servant holds a spontaneous worship service (26-27), as his gratitude bursts forth toward God. As we act in service to God's purposes and for God's people, we experience the reality of God's presence. This becomes the fuel for our worship.

Entering Bethuel's house and seeing Laban's exuberance (29-31), not to mention the comfort after a long journey (32-33), Abraham's servant could have relaxed. But he did not. He trusted God enough to be clear and transparent, repeating the entire story, including every detail. His trust in God allowed him to be clear and honest, not hiding or manipulative. This required faith in God more than desiring a quick resolution or a desired outcome.

Prayer: Father, you want what is best and see everything as it truly is. Help us work with you in faith as we serve your purposes and people today.

One Word: Praise the Lord who works with us

IS IT BECAUSE THERE IS NO GOD IN ISRAEL?

2 Kings 1:1-18
Key Verse 1:3

King Ahab had been wounded and died in battle, as prophesied. Then his son Ahaziah took the throne. When Ahaziah was injured in a fall, he did not seek the Lord, but rather the God of Ekron—Baal-Zebub. The Lord sent his angels to give Elijah a message for the king. "Is it because there is no God in Israel?" King Ahaziah rejected the God of Israel, choosing instead to live as a godless person. He sought help from worthless idols—not the Lord. According to the word of the Lord, he would certainly die. There is no life apart from God.

When King Ahaziah heard the message, he knew it was Elijah. He sent companies of men to bring the prophet, but God protected Elijah, sending fire from heaven to consume the first two detachments. The captain of the third detachment approached Elijah humbly, so Elijah went with him. He told the king that because he did not seek the Lord, but sought the God of Ekron, he would certainly die. Ahaziah died in accordance with the word of the Lord. God is the source of life and blessing in this world. He is the one we must seek in all things.

Prayer: Lord, you are my life in every way. Help me not to seek help from money, fame or worldly things. Protect me from idol worship and help me seek you only.

One Word: Seek the Lord in all things

Monday, March **17**

ELIJAH IS TAKEN UP TO HEAVEN

2 Kings 2:1-11
Key Verse 2:9

Elijah faithfully served God in his lifetime. Now the Lord was about to take Elijah up to heaven in a whirlwind. In preparation, the Lord sent Elijah to different places. Each time Elijah instructed Elisha to stay where he was while Elijah went as the Lord sent him. Elisha refused. He would not leave Elijah at this time. Elijah had been his master, and he knew the Lord was going to take his master from him on this day. They travelled to Bethel, Jericho and finally to the Jordan. Elisha would not leave his master.

When the time came there were fifty men accompanying. Elijah struck the waters of the Jordan, and they parted, enabling Elijah and Elisha to cross—just the two of them. There Elijah asked Elisha what he desired, and Elisha requested something amazing: "A double portion of your spirit." Elijah was taken up to heaven, and Elisha was granted what he asked for. He saw in his master the Spirit that enabled him to prophesy and to suffer for the sake of the Lord. Elisha offered himself to the Lord with this desire.

Prayer: Lord, heal my heart that I may desire to have your Spirit. Help me to serve you and be a spiritual blessing.

One Word: Live with God's Spirit; be a blessing

ELISHA BEGINS HIS MINISTRY

2 Kings 2:12-25
Key Verse 2:15

Elisha witnessed the glory of the Lord when Elijah was taken up to heaven. He tore his clothes and began his new life. He picked up Elijah's cloak, returned to the Jordan and asked, "Where now is the Lord, the God of Elijah?" He struck the waters, just as Elijah had, and the waters parted. The God of Elijah was present., and the spirit of Elijah indeed was resting now on Elisha. The accompanying prophets wanted to search for Elijah, thinking the Lord may have taken him to a mountain or valley somewhere. But Elisha told them not to go. The Lord was now ministering through Elisha.

Elisha came to a town that was situated in a wonderful place, but whose water was foul. Elisha brought healing to the water and to the town. The Lord worked through Elisha to bring healing and life.

There were some who made fun of the prophet and mocked him. Elisha rebuked them for disrespecting his God. Elisha came to restore honor to the God of Israel. He had received a double portion of Elijah's spirit. He used it for the restoration of God's people.

Prayer: Lord, help me to carry on the work of God. Help me to serve God's purpose and pray for the healing and restoration of our nation.

One Word: Minister with God's Spirit

ELISHA TEACHES KINGS TO RELY ON GOD

2 Kings 3:1-27
Key Verse 3:18

When Ahab king of Israel died, Moab revolted against Israel. Ahab's son Joram asked Jehoshaphat king of Judah (his father-in-law) to help him put down the revolt. So, the kings of Israel, Judah and Edom formed a three-way alliance and went to attack Moab. They took a circuitous route through the desert and ran out of water.

In hard times, the one king who believed in the Lord God knew what to do. Jehoshaphat sought out a prophet of the Lord. For the sake of Jehoshaphat, Elisha prayed for them about their water problem. God heard Elisha's prayer and gave them water in the desert. He also promised them victory over the Moabites. The Moabites saw the sun reflected in the water and thought it was blood. The Moabites thought that their attackers had slaughtered each other, so they came to get the plunder and instead, they were completely surprised.

Prayer: Lord, teach me to seek your help and trust you in every crisis.

One Word: The Lord answers his servant

GOD BLESSES TWO WOMEN

2 Kings 4:1-17
Key Verse 4:3

Elisha was met by a woman who was suffering greatly. Her husband, who believed the Lord, had died. Because she had no money, she ended up in debt with no hope of escaping. Creditors threatened to take her two sons and sell them as slaves to pay off the debt. All she had was a small jar of olive oil. Elisha encouraged her to ask for a great blessing. She should request as many jars as she had faith to ask for. Then Elisha miraculously turned her home into an olive oil factory. The small jar of oil was multiplied into enough for her to pay off all her debts. God blessed her according to her faith. We learn to ask for more than just a few.

After this, Elisha met a Shunammite woman. She recognized him as a spiritual leader and shepherd, and she offered him a place to stay in their house whenever he came. Elisha wanted to do something for this generous woman. "What can be done for her?" Learning that she was childless, he promised her that, within a year, she would have a son. She had no such expectation, but God provided her with a son. He blesses with abundance beyond our expectations.

Prayer: Lord, you are a God of blessing. Help me to ask for your blessing with faith. Grant me great expectations based on your mercy.

One Word: Seek God's abundant blessing with faith

ELISHA RAISES THE SHUNAMMITE BOY

2 Kings 4:18-37
Key Verse 4:36

The son of the Shunammite woman grew and was old enough to visit his father when he was working in the fields. One day he complained about a headache. He sat with his mother on her lap, but tragically he died. The woman did not tell her husband, but she took a donkey and hurried after Elisha. Elisha sent his servant to ask if everything was alright, but the woman told him nothing. She went straight to Elisha. She sought God's help through Elisha.

Elisha gave his servant his staff, with instructions to go on ahead and lay the staff on the boy's face, but the boy did not awaken. Then Elisha and the woman arrived. Elisha patiently lay on the boy. The boy grew warm, but did not arise. Elisha paced the floor and tried again. This time the boy sneezed and opened his eyes. Elisha restored the boy to the Shunammite woman, and she bowed and demonstrated her thankfulness. She expressed her personal faith in God by persistently clinging to Elisha, and she was blessed.

Prayer: Lord, only you can give life. Teach me to cling to you and your promise with personal faith in your power and mercy.

One Word: Have personal faith in our life-giving God

ELISHA FEEDS GOD'S PEOPLE

2 Kings 4:38-44
Key Verse 4:44

During Elisha's ministry, there was a severe famine in the region. Elisha was meeting there with some of the other prophets. In their hunger, they collected some herbs and wild gourds to make a stew, not even knowing the ingredients. It smelled so delicious, but it had a bad effect. The men suspected there was something bad or even poisonous in the pot. God's servant Elisha purified it with some flour. This represented his dependence on God. Then the stew in the pot became edible and nourishing.

Another time, a man came bringing Elisha twenty fresh loaves of barley bread, baked from his first ripe grain. It was meant as a gift for Elisha personally. But Elisha instructed his servant to give the bread to the people. The servant objected, because it was not enough for a hundred hungry men. Elisha was sure of God's provision, even in that desperate time. God blessed Elisha's generous heart and his faith in God's abundant provision. The bread became more than enough to feed everyone.

Prayer: Lord, help me to trust you and your provision even when times are bleak. Use me to feed God's people with faith.

One Word: Trust God's provision by faith

NAAMAN IS HEALED OF LEPROSY

2 Kings 5:1-14
Key Verse 5:14

Naaman was a well-respected commander in the Syrian army, highly regarded and valiant. But he had an incurable and humiliating disease: leprosy. Naaman's wife had a servant girl from Israel who knew of Elisha. Though a slave, she believed in the God of Israel. She knew his healing power, and that Elisha was a powerful servant of the Lord. When Naaman sought permission to go to Elisha, the king sent him with a reference letter. The letter implied that the king of Israel should heal Naaman. The king did not trust the king of Aram. He suspected an ulterior motive and tore his clothes.

When Elisha heard of this, he intervened. He instructed Naaman to wash in the Jordan seven times. Then he would be restored. Naaman was proud and became angry. He felt insulted that Elisha did not meet him. He thought there were better rivers than the Jordan to wash in. He became full of rage. Then his servants convinced him to humbly obey. When he did, Naaman was cleansed, and his skin was restored like that of a healthy young boy. God blessed his humble and repentant act of obedient faith.

Prayer: Lord, help me to overcome my idea and my pride. Bless me to humbly obey and be healed.

One Word: Obey God's way and be healed

THERE IS NO GOD EXCEPT IN ISRAEL

2 Kings 5:15-27
Key Verse 5:15

After experiencing God's healing power, Naaman returned to Elisha. He had received more than just healing from leprosy. His spiritual eyes were opened. He met the living God. Naaman showed his gratitude by offering Elisha a gift, but the prophet refused. Naaman then vowed to worship the Lord only. He only asked forgiveness for when he had to join his master at the temple of his god. Naaman was no longer an angry man filled with rage. He was a grateful recipient of God's blessing and a true worshipper of the Lord. He was a new person, healed in every way. Elisha sent him away in peace.

When Gehazi saw the rich gifts which Elisha had refused, he decided that the opportunity was too good to miss, so he ran after Naaman and asked him for a talent of silver and two sets of clothing. He had seen the overflowing blessing of the Lord, but he only sought gain for himself. He tried to conceal what he had done, but God cannot be deceived. As a result of his selfish indulgence, Naaman's leprosy afflicted Gehazi.

Prayer: Lord, help me to worship you only. Protect me from the temptation to gain small things in this world. Help me to know the greatness of your blessing.

One Word: Worship God only

THOSE WHO ARE WITH US ARE MORE

2 Kings 6:1-23
Key Verse 6:16

Elisha's disciples grew in numbers and needed a bigger place. They went to the Jordan to cut logs to build it. One of them lost a borrowed ax head to the river. With the power of God, Elisha made the axe float and solved the problem. A spiritual leader cares for even others' little problems and solves them with God's wisdom and power.

Aram was at war with Israel. The king of Aram plotted to send his troops to seize an important military ground. But each time his plan was foiled because Elisha, with his prophetic intelligence, revealed it to the king of Israel. Knowing the cause of the problem, the king of Aram sent his army to capture Elisha. Elisha saw that God sent His army that was far more and stronger than the Arameans. When Elisha prayed, God struck the Arameans with blindness. Elisha led the enemy soldiers to Samaria and through his prayer, God restored their sight. Elisha asked the king of Israel to set a feast for the Arameans and to set them free. This event revealed God's message to both Israel and Aram that they should open their spiritual eyes to see that God is the Lord of salvation. Having the eyes of faith does not make the problem go away. Those who have the eyes of faith, can see that the Lord is with them and He is much stronger than the problem.

Prayer: Lord, open my spiritual eyes to see your great power and help and to overcome problems.

One Word: Spiritual eyes to see God's salvation

HEAR THE WORD OF THE LORD

2 Kings 6:24-7:2
Key Verse 7:1

The King of Aram laid siege to Samaria, the capital of Israel. The long siege created extreme famine in the city, and the people suffered unspeakably from starvation. As the helpless king of Israel was walking on the wall of the city to inspect conditions, he heard the most horrific and bleakest story of cannibalism. It must have sickened his heart. Yet, instead of turning his heart to God and waiting for God's deliverance, he blamed God and his prophet for the whole affair and wanted to kill Elisha. This is a common response when life becomes very hard and difficult. Prolonged hardships are the times when we need to hold onto God and wait for him to help.

Elisha declared that within a day the siege would be over and there would be plenty to eat. After listening to Elisha, the officer scoffed at Elisha's prophecy. He did not know that human extremity is God's opportunity to demonstrate his power. Elisha assured the officer that the prophecy would come true, but his unbelief would cause him to miss God's miraculous blessing. Failing to believe the promises of God results in failing to receive God's blessings. God's words of promise are meant to be fulfilled. We need to hold onto them and experience God's blessings.

Prayer: Lord, help me turn my heart to you in times of difficulties, hold onto your words of promise, and wait for your help and blessing.

One Word: God can open the floodgates of heaven

LET'S GO AND REPORT GOOD NEWS

2 Kings 7:3-20
Key Verse 7:20

Four starving men with leprosy who lived outside the city gate could neither go inside the famine- stricken city nor stay there to starve to death. They had only one option to go surrender to the Arameans, although there was a slim chance for them to receive the mercy of the enemies. When they came to the Aramean camp, they found it empty of soldiers. God caused the enemies to hear the noise of a great army and to run away leaving everything behind.

The four men with leprosy enjoyed food and treasures. Soon they realized that God had brought the salvation not only to them but to the starving city. They felt they were responsible to share the good new with people in the city. They went back and shouted out the news to the city. God used these outcasts with leprosy to share the good news and to save starving people. Those who encounter the good news, Christ Jesus, are responsible to share it with starving and dying people.

After some careful checking as to the reliability of their testimony, the people went out and plundered the camp. As Elisha prophesied, God saved Samaria, but the unbelieving royal officer was trampled to death. There is a cost to unbelief.

Prayer: Lord, help me to be willing and responsible to share the good news to those who are spiritually starving and dying.

One Word: The Gospel must be shared.

GOD KEEPS HIS PROMISE

2 Kings 8:1-29
Key Verse 8:19

Elisha told a Shunammite woman to leave Israel to escape a seven-year famine. She took her son and did as he told her. After she returned home seven years later, she appealed to the king for her property. As the king was listening to Gehazi who recounted Elisha's work to restore the dead to life, the mother appeared before the king and confirmed the event. She had her property restored and her faith in God rewarded. Jesus is our advocate before God. He will say, "Here is the one I've told you about that I've given him eternal life."

Ben-Hadad was ill and sent his servant Hazael to Elisha to find out if he would survive the illness. Seeing Hazael, Elisha wept, because Hazael would murder his king and become a ruthless enemy king to the Israelites. Sovereign God knows and controls everything. We are to trust God who is ultimately in control, even when evil surrounds us.

Jehoshaphat, a good king of Judah, had his son Jehoram marry Ahab's daughter Athaliah for political advantage. The marriage brought far- reaching adverse results. Athaliah influenced her husband Jehoram and her son Ahaziah toward idol worship and wickedness. The influences of the godly spouse and the parent are critical. God kept his promise to David by not destroying Judah.

Prayer: Lord, you are our Advocate, Sovereign Lord, and merciful God. Help me trust you.

One Word: God keeps his promise

GOD'S JUDGMENT ON THE HOUSE OF AHAB

2 Kings 9:1-37
Key Verse 9:7

Elisha sent a young prophet to Jehu to anoint him king over Israel and to tell him to strike down the house of Ahab. After the prophet had done as he was told, the army officers rallied under Jehu at once and proclaimed him as the king of Israel. In his time, God raised Jehu as his instrument of judgment over the house of Ahab.

During this time, Israel was at war with Aram. Joram king of Israel returned to Jezreel to recover from his battle wounds. Jehu stormed into Jezreel like a madman. Joram did not suspect Jehu's treachery and went out with Ahaziah king of Judah to meet him. At this point Jehu was filled with thoughts of honoring God as an instrument of divine judgment against the house of Ahab. He killed Joram and threw his body onto the land of Naboth. Jehu also killed Ahaziah who had allied with the wicked house of Ahab.

Jezebel was defiant even when judgment and death was on her. Her death fulfilled Elijah's prophecy. Although it took many years for justice to be done, it happened exactly as it had been prophesied. God's judgment will come to idolaters and to a land of idolatry and witchcraft in his time.

Prayer: Lord, our world is full idolatry and evils. Help me to turn away from them and warn the world through Bible study and prayers.

One Word: God's judgment will surely come

JEHU'S SUCCESS AND FAILURE

2 Kings 10:1-36
Key Verse 10:10

Jehu seemed to appear to be obedient to the Lord, but then revealed his self-seeking and half- commitment to God. After killing Joram and Jezebel, Jehu confronted the leading men of Samaria either to choose a new king from among Ahab's sons or to kill them all. They chose the latter and slew them all. Jehu also killed all the acquaintances of Ahab in Jezreel. Through Jehu, the prophecy of Elijah was fulfilled. Apostasy and idolatry call for God's thorough judgment.

Jehu summoned all the worshippers of Baal into the temple of Baal and slaughtered them. His hypocrisy was revealed when he didn't destroy the golden calves which King Jeroboam had set. Jehu probably believed that the Baal worship brought great harm to Israel and that they had to come back to God. Yet to him, it was sufficient to worship God at the temple of golden calves in Bethel and Dan. His half-commitment to God led his people to continue the idol worship. Jehu was a successful failure because he was not careful to keep God's words (31). In his complacency, Jehu followed his own judgment and failed. Great success can tempt us to be proud and self- seeking. It is possible to be used by God greatly, but then to stumble into another sin. We ought to seek God's way by following his words.

Prayer: Lord, help me cast out all the idols from my heart and humbly seek your way wholeheartedly.

One Word: Be careful to keep God's words

MAKING A COVENANT

2 Kings 11:1-21
Key Verse 11:17

When Athaliah, saw that her son Ahaziah was killed, she acted quickly to destroy the whole royal family and take the throne for herself. It seemed that David's kingdom was overthrown by a Baal worshipper. Athaliah ruled Judah not realizing that Joash, one of her grandchildren escaped. Jehosheba, Ahaziah's sister, hid her nephew baby Joash in the temple for six years. She valued the life of a young child and risked her life to save Joash. Satan tried to destroy David's lineage, but God kept his promise through Jehosheba.

In the seventh year of Athaliah's reign, a priest Jehoiada began carrying out a plan to dethrone Athaliah. He revealed Joash the royal prince to the commanders and guards and crowned Joash king of Judah. The people celebrated and accepted his coronation. Jehoiada arrested Athaliah, took her outside the temple, and executed her. Jehoiada made a covenant between the Lord, the king, and the people of Judah that they would obey God and respect God's commands. They were restored as God's people again. They smashed the alters of Baal and idols. God kept his promise to David through people of faith and courage. In times of difficulty, we are to stand on the promises of God and fight a good fight boldy.

Prayer: Lord, Satan tries to destroy God's work, but your promises always prevail. Strengthen me to engage in spiritual warfare.

One Word: People of faith and courage

Made in the USA
Monee, IL
28 December 2024

75440970R00062